DISCARDED CONTENTS

Along the Mekong → p. 84

Trips & Tours → p. 98

Sports & Activities → p. 104

Road atlas → p. 126

DID YOU KNOW?
Timeline → p. 12
Local specialities → p. 26
Books & Films → p. 52
On Apsaras, Lingas and
Nagas → p. 65
Currency converter → p. 115
Budgeting → p. 116
Weather in Phnom Penh
→ p. 118

MAPS IN THE GUIDEBOOK
(128 A1) Page numbers and
coordinates refer to the road
atlas
(U A1) Coordinates for the
map of Phnom Penh on the
inside back cover
Coordinates are also given for
places that are not marked
on the road atlas
Detail maps of Angkor Wat
and Angkor Thom → p. 134
Map Siem Reap → p. 135

INSIDE BACK COVER:
PULL-OUT MAP →

PULL-OUT MAP
(𝓜 A–B 2–3) Refers to the
removable pull-out map
(𝓜 a–b 2–3) Refers to additional inset maps on the
pull-out map

The best MARCO POLO Insider Tips

Our top 15 Insider Tips

INSIDER TIP Temple rubbings – souvenirs from Angkor

Inexpensive, unique and beautiful – temple rubbings make wonderful decorations at home and are also easy to pack into your suitcase → **p. 29**

INSIDER TIP ,Apocalypse Now'

Fall asleep by a jungle river just like Marlon Brando did – and to the sound of lions roaring: you can do it in the Utopia Guesthouse near Kampot → **p. 36**

INSIDER TIP Journey through time to Shanghai

Enjoy the evening in the fabulous Chinese House – fashionable bar, club and gallery in Phnom Penh → **p. 46**

INSIDER TIP Leave your cares behind you

Into the hammock and let the world drift by as you watch the sea – the only resort on Kho Tmei Island near Sihanoukville belongs to two Germans and all of their pets → **p. 55**

INSIDER TIP Play Robinson

Leave the world behind you and enjoy solitude: how about a stay on the (almost) deserted islands of Koh Ta Kiev and Rong Samloem? → **p. 51**

INSIDER TIP Magical circus fun

Children and youths, including many orphans and street urchins, learn how to be clowns, magicians and acrobats, run their own show – and go to school as they should → **p. 70**

INSIDER TIP Travel à la Khmer

Put a diesel motor onto a bamboo frame – and the Bamboo Train is ready to go; the most unusual train on earth (photo above) → **p. 70**

INSIDER TIP Cocktails, golden dragons & co.

Relax over cocktails and the atmosphere of old Shanghai – at Miss Wong's in Siem Reap → **p. 79**

BEST OF ...

GREAT PLACES FOR FREE
Discover new places and save money

● **Water festival on the Mekong**
The *Bon Om Touk* water festival at the end of the rainy season revolves around the masses of water in the gigantic river: cheer on the participants in the colourful (and free) regatta in Phnom Penh (photo) → p. 111

● **In the footsteps of the old king**
Get a taste of glamorous days of the pre-war jet set when you visit the lobby of the impressively renovated *Independence Hotel* in Sihanoukville; and it won't cost a penny → p. 54

● **When bats darken the sky**
The sky above will turn dark when thousands and thousands of bats leave the *Phnom Sampeau Caves* at sunset – an extraordinary natural spectacle, and a free one → p. 72

● **On worms and elegant silk**
Artisans D'Angkor let you look behind the scenes: visitors taking part in the free tour are shown the training centre and the stages of production from the mulberry tree plantation and silkworm breeding to weaving the fabric → p. 77

● **Watch freshwater dolphins for free**
You can watch *river dolphins* from the shore in Kratie: all you need is a little bit of luck and good binoculars; there is no need to pay for the excursion boat → p. 90

● **Breathe in the temple air**
You can visit the two monasteries *Wat Sambok* and *Wat Sambour* near Kratie free of charge; but don't forget to dress appropriately → p. 92

● **Free early-morning sport in front of the Royal Palace**
Forget about the fitness studio: you can take part in *aerobics*, *badminton* and *Tai Chi* along with the other early-morning fitness enthusiasts in front of the Royal Palace in Phnom Penh – even before the sun rises – free of charge → p. 40

●●●● Dots in guidebook refer to 'Best of ...' tips

ONLY IN CAMBODIA
Unique experiences

● *A versatile accessory*
You will come across the versatile, checked krama shawl wherever you go in the country. One of the best places to buy one is at the bustling *Phsar Thmay* market in Phnom Penh → p. 45

● *Characteristic silhouette*
On bank notes, the country's flag and even on a beer bottle – no symbol is more characteristic of the country than the largest building in the ruined city of Angkor: the world-famous, majestic *Angkor Wat* monastery is an absolute must! → p. 61

● *Murderous legacy of the Khmer Rouge*
Remember the approximately 1.5 million Cambodians murdered during the terror regime of the Khmer Rouge on the infamous *Killing Fields* near Phnom Penh → p. 49

● *Delicious: a tarantula snack*
If you ever felt a real need to sink your teeth into a crispy fried, fist-sized tarantula, you can sample this little delicacy in the village of *Skun* (photo) → p. 101

● *Crash course in the Cambodian lifestyle*
Discover the 'kitsch as kitsch can' Cambodians love so much in the *Cambodian Cultural Village* in Siem Reap: from a model of a traditional house you can walk through to a wedding ceremony with all the frills including gifts for the monks and hair-cutting ritual → p. 74

● *Boat tour of the Ramsar Wetlands*
After the end of the rainy season, you can chug through an endless labyrinth of river channels, islands and flooded forests *on the Mekong* north of Stung Treng – a lonely, vast amphibian world → p. 97

● *Spirits and blessings*
There are countless spirits in Cambodia and even tourists will not be able to avoid making a small offering to them – the female guardian spirit *Ya Mao* will protect you on your trip along the coast on the N 4 → p. 99

ONLY IN

BEST OF ...

● *Visit the Emerald Buddha*
This is a major tourist attraction in Phnom Penh and one of the holiest places in the country: You will be dazzled by the gold, diamonds and polished marble in the *Silver Pagoda* in the Royal Palace complex (photo) → p. 41

● *A change of pace at the cinema*
Settle back in your chair in the cinema while the monsoon rain hammers down outside. The *Top Cat Cinema* in Sihanoukville makes this possible, showing high-quality films with Dolby surround sound, popcorn and ice cream → p. 53

● *Gods and kings in stone and bronze*
The originals of the most valuable exhibits from Angkor can be admired in the *National Museum* in Phnom Penh – those in the legendary ruined city are mainly copies → p. 41

● *Open-air feast in the monsoon rain*
There's torrential rain over the Tonle Sap River and the children are still frolicking in the flooded streets! Even then, you will be able to stay high and dry and eat exquisitely in the *Bopha Restaurant* in Phnom Penh – with a view of the never-ending activity on the river → p. 43

● *Heaven for souvenir hunters*
Time simply flies at the *Old Market (Phsar Chas)* in Siem Reap. If the hundreds of stands don't have what you're looking for, stay here a bit longer and continue your hunt at the Night Market → p. 76

● *Teatime in the Grand Hotel*
An excellent way to while away your time on a rainy afternoon is over 'high tea' or coffee and cake in *The Conservatory* in *Raffles Grand Hotel d'Angkor* in Siem Reap – snuggle into the sofas and listen to the pianist → p. 81

RAIN

RELAX AND CHILL OUT
Take it easy and spoil yourself

● *Nirvana on earth – in the spa*
Fragrant aromas, soothing music, warm oil, tender hands – the professional team at the *Frangipani Spa* in Siem Reap know how to pamper and revive the travel-stressed souls and tense muscles of footsore tourists → **p. 78**

● *Soothing boat trip*
Balsam for the soul: you can take in peaceful scenes of everyday life from the deck of an excursion boat as it chugs through the stilt-house and houseboat landscape of the wide *Tonle Sap Lake* near Siem Reap (photo) → **p. 83**

● *From waterfall to waterfall in comfort*
How about taking a *ride on an elephant* near Ban Lung in Ratanakiri? Sitting in the basket, you will sway gently from waterfall to waterfall and the fanning of the pachyderms' enormous ears will even provide pleasant ventilation → **p. 89**

● *1,000-star dinner*
After a candlelight dinner in the *Knai Bang Chatt Boutique Hotel* on the coast at Kep, put your feet up, sink back into the cushions of the sofa and enjoy the tasty cocktails – the sound of the surf and twinkling stars in the sky are included in the price → **p. 39**

● *Island hopping, snorkelling and sunbathing*
Boats sail from Sihanoukville for the *island world off the coast:* let the on-board chef spoil you, lie down on the sundeck and close your eyes and enjoy the voyage to the secluded islands where you will have the beach (almost) to yourself → **p. 51**

● *Journey through time on three wheels*
It might be a bit bumpy, but visiting the sights in Phnom Penh by *cyclo* is still a very pleasant experience → **p. 45**

● *Beastly pedicure*
Be nibbled. The small Garra Rufa fish at *Dr. Fish* will take care of your feet – perfect after a temple tour → **p. 78**

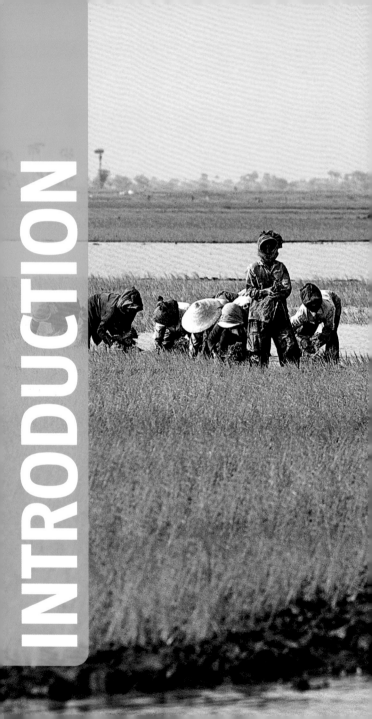

INTRODUCTION

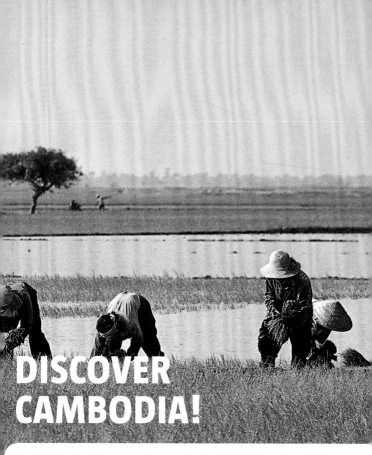

DISCOVER CAMBODIA!

Cambodia is where the sugar palms grow. That is what the Khmer have said since time immemorial. The distinctive, tousled round tops of the palm trees and rice fields cover the surface of the country as far as the eye can see. Water buffalo wallow in the mud, chewing their cud and staring just as they did one thousand years ago. Cambodia is still that way today in spite of the modern countenance of Phnom Penh that all the expats living there have made seem increasingly western. Faced with the hustle and bustle of the Cambodian capital city, it is a good idea to go back to the time before the boom and the karaoke bars, massage parlours and nightclubs.

The fatal year 1975 has never been forgotten in Indochina. First, the Khmer Rouge marched into Phnom Penh and rang in their murderous 'Year Zero'. Two weeks later, the capital of neighbouring Vietnam fell and was renamed Ho Chi Minh City. And finally, the revolution also conquered the sleepy neighbouring country of Laos while the Khmer Rouge under Pol Pot left their own country flooded in a sea of blood. Between one and two million inhabitants were murdered or died under forced labour

Photo: Farmers harvesting rice

It's all go in and out of the water: Serendipity Beach near Sihanoukville

or of hunger. From 1975 to 1979, Phnom Penh was a grim ghost town after it had been forcibly evacuated – until the Vietnamese overpowered the mass murderers in 1979 and made Phnom Penh their command headquarters in what became a satellite state for the next ten years. In the early 1990s, UN soldiers turned the city into something of a wild-west playground where dollars seemed to rain from the sky. Anarchy and chaos, corruption and kidnapping ran riot in Sihanouk's kingdom.

After the 22,000 Blue Berets withdrew from the country at the end of 1993 following the first democratic elections, the solution for Cambodia's future was seen in national reconciliation. The international tribunal against the last living leaders of the Khmer Rouge, which began in 2009, therefore met with little understanding from most of the Cambodians. Under the clique of politicians around Prime Minister Hun Sen (who had once deserted from the Khmer Rouge to the Vietnamese) Cambodia is now enjoying a relatively stable phase of long-awaited peace, but it is also characterised by open corruption at all levels of the administration that is unusual even by Asian standards.

After you leave the capital, you will set out on a journey through time through the real Cambodia. With its 70,000 square miles, the country is around half the size of Germany and your journey will take you over bumpy roads to remote provinces that were once forgotten by the outside world and completely controlled by the Khmer Rouge and malaria. The remote province of Ratanakiri is home to indigenous highland peoples collectively known as the *Khmer Loeu*, who live in the dense forests with their ancient tribal traditions. Neighbouring Mondulkiri is very sparsely populated; the hilly province is largely covered with forests of precious wood and tropical rainforest. Today, a motley assortment of people from all over the world gathers with the Khmer in Sihanoukville – the one more-or-less revived beach resort along 440km (270 miles) of coast – to go for banana-boat rides, play beach volleyball or go island hopping together; in a way, it has developed into a kind of 'Mallorca' for backpackers in Asia.

Depending on the season, the rice fields glow in dazzling green, muddy brown or golden yellow. At first sight, there is idyllic rural

> **At first glance, idyllic rural life wherever you look**

life wherever you look: men and women threshing rice on the fields, the checked *krama* cloth round wrapped around their heads like a turban, their teeth and lips blood red from the juice of betel nuts. Most of the 14 million Cambodians are farmers who live from hand to mouth – an extremely frugal existence between ox carts and stilt houses, their roofs covered with palm thatch, burdened by debt, and rice fields where countless landmines are a constant threat to life and limb. The Kingdom of

March 1992
Start of the UN mission in Cambodia with 22,000 soldiers (UNTAC)

1993
Constitution passed after peaceful elections. Constitutional monarchy under King Sihanouk. UN troops withdraw. The battles against the Khmer Rouge in the north of the country continue

from 15 April 1998
Amnesty and inclusion of most of the Khmer Rouge into the government army after the death of Pol Pot

2004
King Sihanouk abdicates; succeeded by his son Norodom Sihamoni

Cambodia is one of the world's poorest countries with an annual per-capita income of about US $810 (in 2010). In addition to agriculture (rice, cotton, coffee, maize and tobacco), the most important branches of the economy are rubber plantations, fishing, textiles and the timber industry, precious stones and gold, oil and coal.

Buddhist monasteries are the centre of community life

The pagodas are reflected in the lotus ponds near the villages. 90 percent of Cambodians follow Buddhism but animism and ancestral worship are also widespread. The Buddhist temples and monasteries have once again become the social and cultural centre of village communities – as they were before the Pol Pot era when the monks were forced to take off their robes and take their place in the columns of forced labourers (if they managed to escape immediate slaughter in the temples).

According to legend, Cambodia is a country of water. And it's a fact: upstream, the broad Mekong actually turns into vast labyrinth of channels, islands and flooded forests illuminated by the reddish golden veil of the setting sun every evening. Visitors who are brave enough to go out with a fisherman in his longtail boat after the rainy season sometimes find it a bit eerie when they can no longer see the banks of the river through all the trees bent over by the current with fish now swimming in their crowns. The market villages on the Mekong delight with their provincial charm and rare freshwater dolphins. The Cambodians say that the Mekong tributary Tonle Sap is the only river in the world that flows backwards and this has made the Tonle Sap Lake in the middle of the country one of the most fish-rich lakes on the planet. Here the locals live in 'floating villages' on their houseboats and in their stilt houses that occupy the flooded landscape between the water and the sky.

Provincial charm and rare dolphins along the Mekong

The temple city Angkor is the absolute highlight of any trip through Cambodia. Tourists stand in awe before the thousand-year-old towers, gates and pavilions and when

Abundance in the market at Battambang – the area is one of the most fertile in the country

they see the lions and snakes, the dancing asparas and warriors throwing their spears in the gallery corridors. They are testaments in stone to the long-gone advanced civilisation of the idolised Khmer kings, the *deverajas*. The heart of the empire, its ruins now engulfed by the jungle, was in the north of the country. During the dreadful fury of the Khmer Rouge, the temples again fell into a state of hibernation

> **Witnesses to a long-disappeared advanced civilisation**

and, for a long time, it was only possible to safely visit the remote sites as part of a UN convoy – if at all. Today, tourist buses and convoys of tuktuks travel there, and you may even find yourself queuing in the middle of an ancient temple.

Many of the 2.85 million visitors to this once abused country never forget their experience. A country with so many faces – from terrifying grimaces and smiling asparas to Buddha's wise countenance radiating hope.

2011
A further tribunal against three Khmer Rouge leaders – including Nuon Chea, 'Brother Number Two after Pol Pot' – begins

in July 2011
The supreme UN tribunal orders both sides to withdraw their troops after repeated flare-ups of the border dispute between Thailand and Cambodia over the Preah Vihear Temple. It is planned to establish a demilitarised zone around the temple complex

2012
In February, final judgement is passed on the head of the Tuol Sleng torture prison Kaing Guek Eav: life!

WHAT'S HOT

Fashion Street

Fashion Remember number 240. Fashion is at home on the street with this number in Phnom Penh. This is where the New York fashion expert Elizabeth Kiesler has her boutique *Wanderlust (21 Street 240)* and also where you will find Fabrizio Sartor's *Oro Rosso (75 Street 240)*. And you should definitely visit *KeoK'jay*, even though this brand moved out of 240 and into the rooms of a former nightclub in Siem Reap at the end of 2011. *KeoK'jay (The Lane, www.keokjay.org, photo)* promotes the use of environmentally-friendly materials and supports social projects.

Khmer beats

Revival The pre-war hits of *Sin Sisamouth* and *Sereysothea* are being reinterpreted – by the country's up-and-coming musicians. The hip-hoppers *Klap Yahandz (www.myspace.com/klapyahandzproduction, photo)* mix traditional songs with hot beats and Pou Khlaing *(www.myspace.com/poukhlaingmusic)* raps in and about Khmer and has become internationally successful. If you want to experience this musical melange, you should visit *Sharky's Bar (126 Street 130, Phnom Penh)*.

Go down

Underwater Broken chunks of coral and harpooned fish are definitely things of the past in the eyes of the team of *Scuba Nation (in the Mohachai Guesthouse, Serendipity Beach Road, Sihanoukville, photo)*. The diving school offers underwater courses in keeping with its motto of 'explore, conserve, observe'. The team is also involved in cleaning up the ocean floor. *Diving and More (Sopheak Meangul Road, Sihanoukville)* also advocates responsible diving and you can go down below with the guides from the *Eco Sea Dive (www.ecosea.com)* in the Ream National Park.

Non-profit restaurants

Delicious No matter whether Western or Asian dishes, you can really enjoy everything the *Sala Baï (135 Taphul Road, Siem Reap)* has on its menu. An NGO established the restaurant and uses it to train young people from underprivileged families. Street children are given a second chance in the *Friends Restaurant* where they learn how to prepare snacks and typical curries, how perfect service functions, and how to run a restaurant. The restaurant is not the NGO *Mith Samlanh's* first success story. There is also a *Friends Shop (215 Street 13, Phnom Penh)* next door. The *Paul Dubrule School (Airport Road, Siem Reap, photo)* is another organisation that offers budding restaurateurs training opportunities and diners a permanently changing menu with French-Cambodian influences.

Delve deeper

Unspoilt If you want to really discover the country, you should do it in the most natural way possible. *Tara Boat (www.taraboat.com, photo)* takes visitors to the Tonle Sap Lake flood area in traditional canoes. There, you will see floating villages and people who still live in close contact with nature. *Lolei Travel (Siem Reap, loleitravel. com)* will take you from Battambang through rice fields, villages and old railway stations aboard a bamboo train, the so-called *Jungle Express. Pepy Tours (Siem Reap, www.pepytours.com)* lures visitors into the Cambodian hinterland to introduce them to sustainable housing projects, and makes it possible for you to spend the night with the local population and learn something about the region's agriculture.

IN A NUTSHELL

BETEL NUT

You will get used to seeing them in many areas of Asia: the blood-red blobs on the street. But, nobody has been coughing up blood – it's only the juice of the betel nut *(Areca catechu)* a kind of 'everyday drug' similar to our coffee or tobacco. The mouths and teeth of old Cambodians are often stained dark red. The betel nut (which looks a bit like a hazelnut) comes from the betel palm and has a stimulating, and at the same time relaxing, effect. It is ground to a powder, mixed with some slaked lime and then chewed in a betel leaf. The taste is slightly peppery and the residue is spat out. However, consumption of the betel, which is said to be not just a euphoriant but also an aphrodisiac, can colour the teeth, cause diarrhoea and lead to addiction.

BUDDHISM

Murmured *Pali* prayers can be heard coming out of the pagodas. Women in white robes, their heads shaven and hands folded in front of their chest, sit crossed-legged. The clouds of smoke from their joss sticks carry their prayers to the Enlightened One, who started spreading his faith 2,500 years ago in Northern India. The faithful attempt to follow Buddha's teachings in this life in the belief that the cycle of rebirth will one day end in nirvana for them. So they make donations (of money) to the monasteries or directly to the monks, but above all conduct themselves with

Photo: Monks in front of Wat Phnom Monastery

The Cambodians have suffered greatly – but their belief in Buddha and a prosperous future makes them strong

boundless patience and compassion, showing tolerance to all forms of life. Ancestral worship and the belief in spirits are also part of the Cambodian form of Buddhism as is Hindu Brahmanism that found its expression in the godlike veneration of the Khmer kings in the *devaraja* cult starting in the days of the Angkor Empire. Many young men enter a monastery as novices at the start of the monsoon season and practice the 227, partially ascetic, rules of the religious order for a period. The reconstruction of the country is also making headway with the help of Buddha's disciples: 40,000 monks are attempting to fight poverty in villages by making mini-loans available, by informing their countrymen about health care and fostering traditional forms of art.

CYCLOS

The days of these comfortable three-wheelers are numbered. Sluggishly, almost as if in slow-motion, they make their way through the chaotic traffic in

Phnom Penh like relics from times long past. Introduced by the French in 1939, the cyclo drivers are gradually being ousted by mopeds, tuktuks and off-road vehicles. There was nothing they didn't transport in the years when the streets were empty and people were short of cash: entire families, struggling pigs and enough furniture for a whole house! The INSIDER TIP *Cyclo Center (Street 158 | www.cyclo.org.uk)* in Phnom Penh is a kind of self-help organisation with 1,400 members. This is where the drivers can clean their – usually hired – vehicles and learn English; and there have also been cyclo rallies to Siem Reap since 2004.

and forests of precious timber! However, the forests are being rapidly – and illegally – cleared to make way for cashew nut and rubber plantations. The ecologically so important mangrove swamps on the coast are increasingly threatened by charcoal production and shrimp farms. There remains a rich variety of fauna: rare animals, some of which were thought to be extinct, have survived in Cambodia's last natural jungles; they include the Serau mountain goat, brown deer, black bear and Malayan sun bear, rare monkey species, crocodiles and monitor lizards, as well as the legendary national animal of Cambodia, the Kou-

The last of their kind: tigers in the remote border area to Vietnam

There is only one way to avoid this being an obituary: travel by cyclo! Especially around noon and in the side streets, they are relatively safe and offer shade and protection from rain.

FLORA & FAUNA

The country, which was isolated for many years as a result of wars and landmines, has a great number of natural treasures; around two thirds of the remote areas are still covered with jungle

prey wild ox. It is thought that even tigers, leopards, wild elephants and possibly Asian rhinoceroses still roam the dense forests in the country's border regions. Pelicans, herons, cormorants and many other threatened bird species find a bigger choice of fish in Tonle Sap Lake and in the Mekong than anywhere else on earth (around 1,300 species). And, the last freshwater dolphins in Cambodia still splash around in the Mekong (see p. 90).

KHMER PEOPLE

The divine line of the kings of 'Kambuja' was the result of the union between the hermit Kambu and an apsara, a heavenly nymph, named Mera. Their descendants created Angkor under Jayavarman II in the year 802. On his travels in Asia in 1860, the naturalist Henri Mouhout proclaimed that 'it is more magnificent than anything the Greeks or Romans left for us' and asked the Khmer about who had built the ancient temple city. The enigmatic answers ranged from angels to giants and possibly even the Hindu god Indra. Or: maybe it created itself. Mouhout summarised: 'What a sad contrast to the barbarism the country has fallen into today.' The legends and Angkor stood in stark contrast to the image the colonialists and neighbours spread about the Khmer: they were a lethargic people of farmers, fatalistic and subservient. The Vietnamese cursed them as dark-skinned wild people who ate with their hands. The reliefs in Angkor give a perfect depiction of the love of life and the suffering that characterises the history of the Khmer: apsaras with the unfathomable Khmer smile, the 'sourire Khmer', some still with bullet holes from the Civil War, alongside scenes of torture and the chaos of battle. You will see this smile wherever you go in the country: in an impoverished fishing village on the Mekong, on the faces of the musicians in a gamelan orchestra or a shaman conjuring up spirits. And when the Cambodians celebrate one of their festivals, the Khmer smile becomes radiant, as wide as the Mekong, and their gold teeth glitter in the light.

KHMER ROUGE

In the early 1970s, the Khmer Rouge were a group of Communist guerrillas operating in the Cambodian underground, created from the Communist Party of Cambodia. Their reign of terror began on 17 April 1975 when they marched into Phnom Penh. Within two days, the soldiers, many of them still children, forced the evacuation of the city – supposedly, a US bombing attack was imminent. The plan was to establish the perfect Communist society, a nation of rice growers, in 'Democratic Kampuchea'. It was even risky to wear glasses in those days, as intellectuals, monks, teachers and students were murdered, and countless cars, houses, schools, pagodas and statues of Buddha destroyed. The Vietnamese drove out the Communists when they invaded the northern provinces of Cambodia on 7 January 1979. The number of victims of this period of horror that lasted barely four years was staggering: around 1.5 million (almost a quarter of the total population of Cambodia) died as a result of murder, execution, hunger, forced labour and disease. After 'Brother Number One' Pol Pot died unpunished in his jungle hideout in the north of the country in 1998 (he was only subjected to a kind of 'people's tribunal' in his village), the rank and file of the Khmer Rouge were amnestied. The head of the Tuol Sleng torture prison, Kaing Guek Eav, was the first to be brought before an international tribunal in a trial against the surviving band of leaders in 2009. The final verdict was passed in February 2012: life imprisonment for crimes against humanity and war crimes. Other trials have been running since June 2010: against the deputy head of state Khieu Samphan and 'Brother Number Two' Nuon Chea, as well as the former Foreign Minister Ieng Sary and his wife Khieu Thirith (*information: Documentation Center of Cambodia, www.dccam. org*).

KINGS SIHAMONI AND SIHANOUK

Norodom Sihamoni succeeded his 82-year-old father, who is suffering from cancer, in 2004. Trained in ballet and cinematic science (in Czechoslovakia and

Winnowing the rice

North Korea), he was Cambodia's ambassador to UNESCO in Paris from 1993. Until his coronation, the bachelor and aesthete was almost unknown in his own country, and considered politically untarnished; quite in contrast to his two brothers Ranariddh and Sirivudh. In contrast, his father Norodom Sihanouk, known as the 'King-Father of Cambodia', is one of the most colourful characters of our time. He played a major role – in changing alliances – on the international political stage and knew all of the rulers of his age: de Gaulle and Nehru, Tito and Ceausescu, Haile Selassie and Mao Tse Tung. He opposed the USA during the Vietnam War and was ousted in a putsch supported by Washington in 1970. However, Sihanouk continued to pull the strings from his exile in Peking and Pyongyang; he even made a deal with the Khmer Rouge to regain power. Films, books and the – very personal – notes on and by Sihanouk: *www.norodom sihanouk.info.*

LANDMINES

The first thing Reach Uk does when she reaches her place of work in Wat Than in Phnom Penh is take her left leg off. 'It's more comfortable like this', she says with a smile. Then she swings herself behind her loom. Reach Uk is just one of the around 40,000 amputees in Cambodia. Especially along the 700 km (440 mi) border to Thailand in the north-western provinces of Battambang and Pursat, the Vietnamese (from 1979) and Cambodians laid between 1,000 and 3,000 mines per kilometre – the densest minefield on earth! The countless unexploded bombs and missiles from the Vietnam War (the USA dropped more than 2 million tonnes of bombs on Cambodia and Laos) are also a permanent peril and kill more people than the mines – particularly near the Vietnamese border in the east of the country.

Around 4,000 deminers have been working with detectors, shovels and brushes for the *Cambodia Mine Action Centre* (CMAC) and other organisations since 1993; this includes removing mines from temples in Phnom Kulen, Koh Ker and elsewhere. The number of accidents has decreased by about 90 percent since the mid-1990s. But, every day at least one more Cambodian is maimed as a result of stepping on a landmine or bomb relic, and 250 people are still killed in this way each year.

RICE

Literally translated, in Cambodian 'eating' means 'eating rice' *(nyam bay)*. It is amazing just how much can be conjured up from this staple food: bread, cakes and desserts, wine and schnapps, cooking oil, soap and candles, and even roofs of rice straw. The only way the Angkor kings were able to preserve their realm was through extensive rice cultivation and ingenious irrigation technology: they provided nourishment for their 1 million subjects with as many as three harvests each year (today, ineffective irrigation, outdated cultivation methods and drought have reduced this to only two harvests). This labour-intensive grain governs the annual rhythm, and not just for the rice growers: there are legends, harvest festivals and even the rice god. The checked pattern of the rice fields is anything but idyllic for those who have to work them: the grains have to germinate before they can be planted, the sprouts are planted individually into the wet ground where the water level has to remain constant for them to mature. The harvest follows three to six months later. The ears shine golden yellow, the farmers swing their sickles and thresh the grain from the sheaves – in many regions this work is still performed manually. And, before the rice can be cooked, it has to be husked.

Photos of victims of the Khmer Rouge

VOLUNTOURISM

Approximately 2,000 Non-Governmental Organisations (NGOs) – around a quarter of all those registered worldwide! – have established offices in Cambodia since the 1990s. It has been a major trend and one that has now developed into a booming business. Young travellers have become increasingly interested in 'voluntourism', a mixture of volunteer work and tourism. Language training, helping out in orphanages, developing playgrounds, football training and work with handicapped people are among the most popular fields. However, you can't just walk into one of these institutions without any language skills and background knowledge – also about Cambodian life and customs – and ask for a job. Those interested should be careful not to fall into the hands of shady organisations that want to get large sums of money for administration or accommodation in advance. *conCERT Cambodia (connecting Community, Environment and Responsible Tourism, www. concertcambodia.org)* is a good first point of contact for finding some kind of orientation in the jungle of NGOs active in the country and information on responsible organisations in all fields.

FOOD & DRINK

A short stroll through the markets will reveal a lot about the eating habits of the Khmer: roasted rats, grasshoppers on a spit, fried spiders and beetles, the eggs of sour ants and chicken embryos straight out of the egg...

But don't worry: the Cambodians' staple diet consists of rice and fresh fish. Over the centuries, the neighbouring countries have contributed to enriching the country's culinary repertoire – especially the Thais with their, greatly toned-down, curries and the Chinese with noodle soup. The Vietnamese brought their spring rolls and elephant-ear fish with them and the French colonialists left the baguette *(num pang)* – often served as a snack with a tasty filling of eggs, cucumber or sardines.

The Cambodians have a great liking for fish *(trey)* in all variations: smoked or dried as a crispy snack, fried or grilled. Many Khmer eat *num banh choc*, a fish soup with rice noodles, or *kuei tiou*, noodle soup with beef, chicken or pork, for breakfast. Vegetarians should order *Kuei Tiou Bun Lai.* Unfortunately, the noodle soup served along the country roads is often now an instant product fresh from the pack – a fast-food trend that will hopefully not go too far.

In restaurants, several dishes are always served at the same time – the more guests, the more lavish the meal. For example, one orders meat or poultry (in simple eateries, these are usually served complete with their bones and gristle) or fresh fish and seafood if you are near a

Photo: A tasty dish of Prahok Ang

Curry, spring rolls and French baguettes – the neighbours and colonial masters have influenced Cambodia's cuisine

river or the coast. Small spring rolls – fried *(num chaio)* or made of white rice paper *(naim)* – filled at the table with carrots and mushrooms are a popular starter. The main vegetables, cabbage, mushrooms, maize and bamboo sprouts are often just cooked briefly in a wok before being served.

A soup *(samlor)* is a must at every meal; either with chicken *(moan)*, beef *(sa-ich koa)* or pork *(sa-ich chrouk)*. Salads have nothing in common with lettuce and co. but are made out of raw beef and typical

herbs, or green, unripe mangos with smoked fish or shrimps. The basic ingredient of the curries *(kari)* is a paste made out of aromatic lemongrass, chilli, garlic and ginger ground in mortar and then cooked in a wok with vegetables and meat in coconut milk. The colour is no indication of the spiciness. The red curry is mild and rather sweet (red *mkak* seeds provide the colour) and the Khmer also consider sweet potatoes essential ingredients. Other frequently used spices include coriander, mint, lemon leaves, star

LOCAL SPECIALITIES

▶ **Amok** – fish or chicken in coconut milk, with garlic, ginger, lemongrass, chilli and curcuma, served in a basket of banana leaves or half a coconut (photo left)

▶ **Kampot Pepper Crab** – crabs with the world's best green pepper

▶ **Kari Baitongh Saich Moan** – green chicken curry with coconut milk sauce

▶ **Loc Lac** – beef dish with garlic and onions in a lime marinade, usually served on lettuce leaves

▶ **Naim** – vegetarian spring rolls of white rice paper filled with various (raw) vegetables (photo right)

▶ **Num Chaio** – small fried spring rolls with minced meat and vegetables

▶ **Nyoum Trayong Chek** – salad of banana flowers, often with chicken, lemon sauce, Thai basil and pieces of peanuts

▶ **Plia Saich Koa** – salad of slices of raw beef with vegetables and herbs such as lemongrass, coriander and mint

▶ **Prahet Trey Chean (fishcake)** – small fried balls of fish filet, vegetables and lemongrass; delicious when served with a dip as a starter

▶ **Saich Koa Char Spee Khieu** – slices of beef fried in a wok with onions, garlic and Chinese broccoli in a rich sauce

▶ **Samlor Kako** – vegetable soup, usually with sweet potatoes, beans, pumpkin, seasoned with lemongrass, curcuma and fish sauce; also served with fish or chicken

▶ **Samlor Macho Boang Koang** – clear, slightly sour shrimp soup, spiced with lemongrass, coriander and Thai basil, inspired by the Thai classic Tom Yam; also served as chicken soup *(Samlor Macho Saich Moan)*

▶ **Trey Dom Rey** – fried elephant-ear fish in sweet-and-sour sauce

aniseed, tamarind and taro root. The **INSIDER TIP** *Khmer Barbeque,* in which meat and vegetables are cooked in sizzling soup in a clay pot above a glowing charcoal fire, is also very popular – you should definitely try it! Cambodians often season their food with the notoriously salty fish paste *prahok* – something that western palates (and noses) can find difficult to get used to; however, a less pungent version is usually served in better restaurants.

The Cambodians even conjure up their cakes and desserts out of rice: for example, sticky rice with black beans sweetened with coconut milk and palm sugar, and either baked in bamboo cane or rolled in banana leaves. Other popular snacks served on the wayside include relatively hard slices of still unripe mangos *(sway)*. Of course, there are also soft, sweet mangos *(sway tum)* in the season from March to May. And, you should not overlook all the exotic fruits such as the red-spiked rambutan, the pink dragonfruit, the juicy mangosteens, the papayas, pineapples and small, sweet bananas.

Coffee is usually drunk black or with sweetened condensed milk. Many restaurants serve tea to accompany your meal as soon as you have been seated. You can enjoy fruit juice *(toek kalok)* anytime and anywhere (but avoid the egg yolk), or you might prefer freshly pressed sugarcane juice drunk with a straw out of a carton. If you feel thirsty, you should avoid the ubiquitous stalls with fanta bottles – they sell petrol! The local alcoholic beverages include Angkor Beer and palm wine *(toek thnaout:* the fermented sweet-sour juice of the sugar palm). Of course, you will find soft drinks, wine, western beer, whiskey and vodka in all of the tourist centres – and it will be difficult to choose between the countless restaurants with international cooking: from pizza to couscous to sushi. There is probably a good reason for the Cambodians' love of fried tarantulas, water beetles and similarly exotic delicacies: under the Pol Pot regime, it is likely that this kind of food saved many of the Cambodians forced to work in the fields from starvation.

And, by the way: in Cambodia, people eat with a spoon and fork as they do in Thailand. Chopsticks are only used along with a spoon when eating noodle soup. *Angchean tchnang!* Enjoy your meal!

Mobile kitchen at the market

SHOPPING

You should count on having to pay for excess baggage when you fly home from Cambodia: the range of arts and crafts and other souvenirs is great, particularly in Siem Reap and Phnom Penh. Bargaining is the order of the day at the markets – but don't forget to smile! You will get the best deals early in the morning or just before the shops close. Many shops donate their profits to humanitarian projects or send them directly back to the villages where the goods were produced. Only experts should think seriously about buying gems from the area around Pailin – there are too many overpriced (glass) bargains on sale.

CAMBODIAN SILK

The sought-after silk is produced in various qualities and sold as fashionable clothing, sarongs, cushion covers and purses. You will be able to get an idea of the entire process of silk production from the mulberry tree to the harvest to the loom if you visit the *National Silk Center* or *Angkor Silk Farm* near Siem Reap. The greedy silkworms are fed the leaves of the mulberry trees before pupating into roughly thumb-size cocoons surrounded with a single strand of up to 1,000 metres in length. The threads unravel when they are boiled in large kettles and are then coloured, washed, spun, straightened once again and wound onto spools. Finally, the silk fabric is produced on the looms using the *ikat* method: Before weaving, the silk thread is died a different colour every 2cm. The weaver needs to have excellent eyesight to be able to produce a balanced pattern.

CULINARY ARTICLES

What would Parisian restaurants do without pepper from Kampot? Spices and honey, coffee and tea, cashew nuts, rice wine and coconut oil, as well as unique products made of sugar palm and water hyacinth – you will probably not want to stop sniffing, searching and tasting when you visit a market.

HANDICRAFTS

Statues of all sizes and colours, baskets and rattan furniture, pottery and lacquerwork, traditional musical instruments and shadow-theatre figures are available at reasonable prices in all of the tourist centres. The popular copies of apsaras,

You can hunt through Cambodia's markets and boutiques for days – and buy wonderful souvenirs to take home with you

Buddhas, Hindu gods and the old god-kings such as wisely smiling Jayarvaman VII are usually made of stone, bronze or wood; a polychrome technique is then used to give the works of art a deceptively genuine patina. *Artisans d'Angkor (www.artisansdangkor.com)* in Siem Reap offer tours of their workshops. Make sure the dealer clarifies that you can get an export license from the Fine Arts Department in Phnom Penh if you buy any (often only seemingly) genuine antiques and also that air shipment can be arranged if necessary.

KRAMA SHAWLS

The classic Cambodian souvenir: the *krama* shawl in red, blue or black checks is made of pure, hand-spun cotton – it is an inexpensive all-round accessory (from 50 cents/3,000 riels) for use on dusty country roads and in ice-cold restaurants, as a towel or to cover your shoulders when you visit a pagoda.

SILVER

Cambodian silversmiths create works of the highest quality and purity (allegedly 70 to 92 percent; but there are also any number of well-made copies). How about jewellery and Buddha statues, chopsticks and cutlery as souvenirs? The small silver *areca nut* containers shaped like animals or fruit, which were formerly used to store betel nuts to take the edge of one's hunger, have developed into a real hit. Small silver anklets for babies, the INSIDER TIP *Chang Krang Cheung*, are especially popular with Khmer parents.

TEMPLE RUBBINGS

Prints from Angkor Wat, or of the Ramayana myth, on heavyweight (rice)paper treated with moisture make INSIDER TIP *practical souvenirs*: easy to transport, inexpensive and exceedingly beautiful.

THE PERFECT ROUTE

FROM THE CAPITAL TO THE PROVINCES

Leave **①** *Phnom Penh* → p. 40 on the A 6 and travel to the northwards past **②** *Skun* → p. 101. This is where the brave can sink their teeth into exotic delicacies such as grilled tarantulas. The N7 turns off towards the Mekong beyond Skun. Before you cross the gigantic river over a long bridge in **③** *Kampong Cham* → p. 107, you can enjoy the sight of the large Buddhas and copies of buildings in Angkor on the nearby temple hill of Phnom Proh. On your way north, take the shortcut via Chhlong directly along the river.

ALONG THE MEKONG

You can follow the Mekong along the N7 in your car. However, it is much more fascinating to charter a boat. With a little bit of luck, you might even be able to see one of the last Irrawaddy freshwater dolphins near **④** *Kratie* → p. 90. Not far away, one of the largest temples in the country, **⑤** *Wat Sambour* → p. 92 (photo left), is well worth visiting. Continue along the N7 for 120km (75mi) until you reach remote, charmingly sleepy **⑥** *Stung Treng* → p. 96. Wouldn't a bicycle ride along the riverbank be a good idea now?

ADVENTURE IN THE EAST

Your route now takes you eastwards along the bumpy N78 to Ratanakiri. The adventurous will find plenty to keep them on their toes in the area around the province capital **⑦** *Ban Lung* → p. 85: you can encounter wild animals on a trekking tour in the **⑧** *Virachay National Park* → p. 89, bathe under spectacular waterfalls, and witness ancient tribal rituals in the Khmer Loeu villages. When you reach Mondulkiri in the south, drive back along the N7 towards Snuol, and then turn off towards the east along the motorway-wide track into the highlands. When you reach the province capital **⑨** *Sen Monorom* → p. 93, you can visit Cambodia's highest waterfall, an elephant project and the villages of the Phnong highlanders.

ON THE TRAIL OF THE KHMER KINGS

Take the same route back to Kampong Cham and turn northwards towards **⑩** *Kampong Thom* → p. 102, a good place to spend the night. You then continue along the N6 to **⑪** *Siem Reap* → p. 73. This is the starting point for excursions to the mythical ruined city

Experience the many facets of Cambodia from the north to the south with some detours to out-of-the-way provinces

of **12** *Angkor* → p. 57 (photo right) with its world-famous temple complexes. If you feel hungry when you get back to Siem Reap, you should try some Khmer cuisine. How about a cooking course while you are there? In the rainy season, you can cruise along channels to tranquil, charming **13** *Battambang* → p. 68; by car, take the N6 and N5.

ON THE SOUTH COAST

The more intrepid can make the return trip by boat across the endless waters of **14** *Tonle Sap Lake* → p. 83 but it is more comfortable to drive back to Phnom Penh along the N6. On your way back to the coast via the N2 and N3, you should stop at the picturesque river hamlet **15** *Kampot* → p. 33, and set out for the **16** *Bokor High Plateau* → p. 36 early in the morning. Mist usually blocks the panoramic view from more than 900m (3,000ft) soon after midday

BATHING AND ISLAND HOPPING ON THE COAST

Relax and enjoy life on the beach in **17** *Sihanoukville* → p. 49: locals and tourists have fun on the beaches, boats set out for the many islands in the Gulf of Thailand. The adventurous reach the former smugglers' island of **18** *Koh Kong* → p. 54 with its mangrove forests, beaches and rivers via the N48. You drive back to Phnom Penh from Sihanoukville along the N4 with a possible detour to visit the **19** *Kirirom National Park* → p. 98.

2,600km (1,600mi). Recommended duration: 3–4 weeks (with a hire car and driver) Driving time: approx. 50 hours Detailed map of the route on the back cover, in the road atlas and the pull-out map.

PHNOM PENH & THE COAST

There can be no doubt about it: **Phnom Penh has cast off its beggar's clothes. Many of the weatherworn ochre-yellow colonial buildings from the French era have been spruced up and are now run as extremely elegant hotels and lounge bars where the guests are welcomed by the lilac blossoms of the bougainvilleas and creaking rattan chairs.**

The times when the city turned into a Kafkaesque, unreal scene of flickering candlelight and open fires in front of the housing barracks, with the sound of generators droning in the background and – not infrequently – pistol shots ringing out, now seem far away. It was still like that in the mid-1990s. Attempts at *coups d'état* were the order of the day.

Today, Phnom Penh glitters like a Christ-mas tree: garlands of lights hang like sparkling tinsel on the hotels, temples and the palm trees lining the lively promenade along the banks where the Tonle Sap and Mekong converge. There is electricity once again (since 1995) and street lamps (since 1998) and even neon advertising signs and digital traffic lights which let you know how many seconds you have left to cross the street. In the evening, it seems as if the city's 1.5 million inhabitants have all gathered for *dalin* – to see and be seen in an endless armada of mopeds cruising the streets without a goal. After a lap of honour around the Independence Monument, the people of Phnom Penh head for one of the countless Khmer inns. Their names are real tongue twisters but express the desires of

Photo: Victory Beach near Sihanoukville

The streets of the Cambodian capital have come back to life – and what was formerly Indochina's Riviera once again attracts bathers

all the Khmer: freedom, equality and health. For young people, that means: mobile phones, mopeds and karaoke. As in the years before 1960, well-to-do Phnom Penhois are drawn to the beaches between Sihanoukville and Kep. The distance from the Thai to Vietnamese border is around 440km (275mi) and the first boutique hotels and casinos have already opened their doors on what used to be 'Indochina's Riviera'. While Sihanoukville seems to be developing more and more into a bustling international seaside re-

sort, time seems to have stood still in the small towns of Kampot and Kep – it's just a question of how long this will last because there are jungle national parks, with wild animals, caves and waterfalls on the coast just waiting to be explored.

KAMPOT

(132 C5) (*Ø G6*) **The atmosphere of the colonial period can still be felt in this tranquil little town on the Toek Chhouu**

River with its groves of palm trees along the riverbank promenade lined with small houses with shady arcades and rickety blue shutters.

Back in the 19th century Kampot had a flourishing harbour with Chinese merchant ships and pastel-coloured shophouses. Today, it is around 5km (3mi) inland, surrounded by mangrove forests and swamps. Most of the city's 40,000 inhabitants live from crabbing, the pep-

Makara Street with their beautiful old, pastel-coloured buildings that are slowly fading. Take a closer look and you'll discover real feasts for the eyes such as the **INSIDER TIP** tiny Chinese shophouse with the oval art-déco windows under a dilapidated tiled roof (visible the roof of the *Bar Red*, a popular place for night owls late in the evening). The *Khmer Cultural Development Institute*, where young people perform Khmer dances

Fishermen selling groceries: small shops at the harbour in Kampot

per plantations and cultivating the notorious, stinking durian fruit. Kampot is a popular place from which to embark on trips to the Bokor National Park, 41km (25mi) to the north – or as a stop-off on the way to Vietnam which is just 50km (31mi) away.

SIGHTSEEING

Strolling around town you'll get a sense of the tranquil colonial atmosphere, especially along the eastern river bank with its magnificent governor's residence and in the alleyways to the south of *Seven*

and play traditional instruments provides a fascinating insight into customs that have been handed down for generations *(Mon–Fri 7–11am and 2–5pm; 6.30–7.30pm only dance, 7.30–9pm only music | a donation is appropriate)*.

FOOD & DRINK

In the evening, it can be hard to find a place to sit along the riverbank – this is where people get together at sunset in the bars and restaurants. Foodies are drawn to *Fruit Shake Street* where the cookshops between the old bridge and roundabout sell the most exotic varieties of fruit juice imaginable, as well as noodle soup and snacks.

EPIC ARTS CAFÉ ☺

This small café is run by young deaf people and the British Epic Arts organisation. You put crosses next to the things you want to order on a slip of paper: breakfast, bagels and muesli, omelettes and other snacks. It is also possible to buy arts and crafts and handmade postcards here. *Daily | 67 Ekareach St. (1st May Road, near the old market Phsar Granath) | www.epicarts.org.uk | Budget*

RIKITIKITAVI ☇

Good restaurant with a veranda, unusual dishes and large servings (e.g. breakfast, imported steaks and vegetarian food), good wines, cocktails and whiskies, and a beautiful river view. *Daily | esplanade in the centre | tel. 012 23 51 02 | Budget– Moderate*

TA EOU ☇

A restaurant on stilts above the river, where you can enjoy the finest fresh seafood as well as a magnificent view. The tourist groups who sometimes drop in have given the Ta Eou the reputation of being expensive; but don't worry: many Khmer also eat here (dishes from around 15,000 KHR). A delicious shrimp starter, tea and bananas are even included in the price! *Daily | esplanade near the new bridge | Budget*

SPORTS & ACTIVITIES

For those who have enough time and want to participate and not just look on: many kinds of volunteering are very popular in Kampot. These include teaching English to the monks, projects with handicapped orphans (see: Epic Arts Café), or even football training. Angela in the popular *Blissful Guesthouse* will give you all the information you need *(esplanade in the centre of Kampot | tel. 092 49 43 31 | www.blissfulguesthouse.com).*

BOAT, KAYAK AND CYCLE TOURS

Kayaks can be hired at Les Manguiers (see below); costing around 15,000 KHR for two hours, this is a good way of observing everyday life on the Chhouu and seeing how the crabbers go about their work. Or, how about a sunset cruise to

MARCO POLO HIGHLIGHTS

★ **Bokor National Park**
Mysterious in the rainy season; at other times a fabulous panoramic view of the coast near Kampot → p. 36

★ **Knai Bang Chatt**
The most beautiful boutique hotel in Cambodia, constructed in the style of Le Corbusier, is located in Kep → p. 39

★ **Silver Pagoda (Royal palace)**
Pomp and splendour in the heart of Phnom Penh: marble, silver, 2,086 diamonds – and a life-sized Buddha made of 90 kg of pure gold → p. 41

★ **Sunset cruise on the Mekong**
Not only for young lovers: experience sunset on the river in Phnom Penh! → p. 46

★ **Raffles Le Royal**
You can't spend the night more stylishly than here – in this colonial hotel with its legendary Elephant Bar → p. 48

the Tek Chhouu Rapids *(8km/5mi north)* and a dip in the river to cool off? Private charter approx. 35,000 KHR/hour *(tel. 092 17 42 80)* or from Sok Lim Tours *(tel. 012 71 98 72 | www.soklimtours.com).*

ENTERTAINMENT

BAR RED
Classic bar to hang out in at night: Steve the Welshman serves Khmer rice dishes, Indian food such as Chicken Masala and, of course, beer, shakes and tea in a laid-back atmosphere between the bar and rattan chairs – open-ended until well after midnight. *Daily from 6pm | Street 718, on the corner of Seeing Hands Massage, approx. 30m from the esplanade*

WHERE TO STAY

LES MANGUIERS ✨
The Manguiers is located right on the river. It has simple rooms (ceiling fan, some with shared bathrooms, cold water) in typical stilt houses with panoramic views – also suitable for families – and six traditional bungalows roofed with palm fronds in the garden. Absolutely delicious homemade breakfast, and it's possible to swim in the river! *13 rooms | esplanade | around 2km along the gravel road north of the new bridge | tel. 092 33 00 50 | www.mangokampot.com | Budget–Moderate*

MEA CULPA
This peaceful little inn offers good value for money: pleasant, bright rooms (DVD, hot-water shower, one room has a balcony), shared veranda, well run and hospitable. The restaurant serves pizza from a wood-burning oven. *4 rooms | River Road | at the south end of the esplanade, turn left behind the governor's villa | tel.*

012 50 47 69 | www.meaculpakampot. com | Budget

INSIDER TIP ▶ UTOPIA
You can relax for a few days at Max's – right over the river that here is overgrown with jungle – and feel like Colonel Kurz/Marlon Brando in 'Apocalypse Now' (at night, you will even hear tigers roaring – not really; they're actually the two lions in the nearby zoo). You have a choice between dormitory beds (with safe, towel, mosquito net) and five simple rooms (not suitable for people more than 1.70m/5ft 7in tall!) and two wonderful – albeit rather spartan – stilt bungalows with veranda (cold-water shower, ceiling fan). Fabulous: you can swim in the river! *7 rooms | 8km (5mi) north of Kampot | tel. 012 40 73 05 | utopiakampot. blogspot.com | Budget*

WHERE TO GO

BOKOR NATIONAL PARK ★
(132 C5) (Ø F–G 5–6)
The Bokor National Park (also: *Preah Monivong*) covers an area of around 1,600 sq km (620 sq mi) on a precipitous high plateau in the heart of the *Elephant Mountains*. In the 1920s, rich Cambodians and colonialists liked to spend their weekends on the 1,080m (3,500ft) high Phnom Popok: today, the overgrown ruins in the *Bokor Hill Station* still give an impression of those opulent days: the Black Palace of the royal Sihanouk family, a French church, an old hotel villa, the post office, the water tower and the once bombastic four-storey casino (*Bokor Palace* dating from 1925) – with its open fireplace and breathtaking view of the coast as far as the Vietnamese island of Phu Quoc. A little way away is the tiny *Wat Sampeau Doi Moi* with its charming brick pagoda and five monks.

Dense jungle in the Bokor National Park – a threatened haven for endangered animals

In the 1980s and 1990s, the Khmer Rouge hid from the Vietnamese troops in the surrounding forests. A footpath, just 2km long, takes visitors to the *Popok Vil Waterfall* with its two approximately 15 m (50 ft) high cascades (*10km/7mi north of Bokor Hill Station; only worthwhile in the rainy season*). The fauna and flora not only includes 300 bird species but also muntjac deer, Asian black bears, gibbons, elephants and tigers – unfortunately still threatened by illegal hunting. Now that the mines have been cleared, Bokor Hill and the casino, which is in danger of collapsing, have once again become a popular destination for excursions and picnics and, especially on holidays, families from all provinces make their way here. An outright megalomaniac hotel-casino project with several Las Vegas-style high-rise resorts is planned.

In the rainy season and after midday when the mist descends there is a wonderfully spooky atmosphere among the ruins, which in 2002 provided the setting for the final showdown in the sinister thriller 'City of Ghosts' with Matt Dillon. *41km (25mi) north of Kampot | trekking tours: Sok Lim Tours (see above) | bunk beds in dormitories available from the rangers in the Bokor Hill Station | admission 20,000 KHR*

TEK CHHOUU FALLS (132 C5) (*ⓜ G6*)
especially at the weekend, this stretch of rapids around 8km (5mi) north of Kampot attracts masses of Cambodians who come here to swim in the pools or have a picnic. Many stalls take care of those who do not bring their own food. There is also a small private zoo on the way.

KEP

(132 C6) (*ⓜ G6*) **This village with 10,000 inhabitants experienced its heyday as a summer resort during the French colonial era: Kep-sur-Mer.**
The royal family also came here to amuse themselves in the water and at the roulette table. The Khmer Rouge put an end to all elitist fun and games in 1975 and almost completely destroyed the hated

stronghold of the bourgeoisie. The nightmare continued in the ghost town until the mid-1990s. Today, Kep is still a wonderfully sleepy place during the week but springs to life at weekends when whole clans of locals pour in to have a picnic or go for a swim in the sea. There has even been talk about a pier for cruise ships, casino and golf course. One thing is certain: the promenade along the shore revolves around just one theme – crab boats, the crab market and a gigantic bronze crab. *Information: www.kepcity. com*

SIGHTSEEING

ROYAL VILLAS

Ex-King Sihanouk's modern, deserted weekend villa *(Damnaksdach)* crowns a hill above the beach at Kep and is now almost completely overgrown. A second, less well-known royal villa around 3km to the east on the coast road is more impressive: a colonial building with a gar-

den, frescoes on the façade and sweeping staircase in the interior where the ex-soldier Mr Teiv lives (he charges an admission fee of 4,000 KHR). The bullet holes in the façades of other ruined villas give an idea of the savagery of the Khmer Rouge.

FOOD & DRINK

Sunset is the ideal time for you to try the delicious specialities served by the many soup kitchens at the crab market *(Phsar Gadam)* or on platforms and raffia mats at *Kep Beach*: especially squid, shrimps and skewered fish cooked over a charcoal grill, as well as *Kampot Pepper Crab*, which is also served at *Kim Ly Loka (Budget)* at the crab market.

LE FLAMBOYANT

Chic garden restaurant with Mediterranean-French-Cambodian cuisine prepared using organic ingredients; the restaurant cultivates its own vegetables.

Exquisite seafood fresh from the net: crab market in Kep

Daily | turn inland on the N33 after Kampot | tel. 016 71 38 23 | *Moderate*

BEACHES & SPORTS

Kep's beaches are unfortunately greyish brown, stony and not really up to western standards; it's a better idea to take a day trip, including seafood lunch and snorkelling *(25,000–50,000 KHR/person)*, to one of the seven islands off the coast, such as the tiny 2 sq-km (500-acre) *Koh Tonsay* with beach restaurants and spartan huts available from the fishermen's families *(electricity 7–10pm | Budget)*.
You can combine your island-hopping tour with *Koh Svay (Mango Island)* or *Koh Pos (Snake Island)*. If you go snorkelling, you won't see much coral (except near *Koh Saran)* but a lot of spectacularly coloured fish. The largest island *Phu Quoc* belongs to Vietnam (25km/16 mi away) and can be reached via the Ha Tien border crossing; get your visa in advance. Ferries set sail from there every day. The Sailing Club next to Knai Bang Chatt has all the equipment needed for catamaran sailing, windsurfing and kayaking *(15,000 KHR/hour)*.

ENTERTAINMENT

KUKULUKU BEACH CLUB

Things really get lively every Friday night in the small guesthouse *(3 rooms; dormitory)* with the air-conditioned bar and small (grey) beach: swing to the latest rhythms around the pool and barbecue. *On the N33 after Kampot | tel. 012 60 78 77 | www.kukuluku-beachclub.com*

WHERE TO STAY

THE BEACH HOUSE

Centrally located but still quiet, with cheerful, comfortable rooms. Shared veranda with a fabulous view of the sun setting into the sea (1st floor), mini-pool and spa, WiFi. *16 rooms | on the seafront | tel. 012 71 27 50 | www.thebeach housekep.com | Moderate*

KEP LODGE ⠧

Various sizes of stone and stilt bungalows with thatched roofs, enjoying spectacular views on the slopes of the Bokor Mountains. Small saltwater pool and billiards; informal restaurant with Swiss specialities such as fondue and rösti on the menu *(Moderate)*. A lot of information on tours. Book well in advance! *6 rooms | turn inland from the N33 after Kampot | tel. 092 43 53 30 | www.keplodge.com | Budget–Moderate*

KNAI BANG CHATT ★

Consisting of two Le Corbusier-style villas from the 1960s, this exclusive and intimate establishment was the first boutique hotel on the coast. Accommodation is in minimalist rooms (without TV) and there is a beautiful slat water infinity pool right by the beach. In the restaurant you can dangle your feet in the still-warm sand and watch the sun go down while you ● INSIDERTIP▶ dine by candlelight, before enjoying a cocktail sprawled across a plush sofa under the starry sky. *11 rooms | on the N33 to Kampot | reservations in Phnom Penh | tel. 023 21 21 94 and 078 88 85 56 | www.knaibangchatt. com | Expensive*

VERANDA NATURAL RESORT ⠧

Bungalows perfect for families and a villa on the slopes: a great deal of wood, natural stone and terracotta, some hammocks on the terrace and open-air baths, rustic but luxurious! Restaurant *(Budget)* with fabulous panorama of the coast at sunset, bakery and ice-cream production. Often completely booked up. *20 rooms |*

*turn inland from the N33 after Kampot |
tel. 033 39 90 35 | www.veranda-resort.
com | Moderate–Expensive*

WHERE TO GO

PHNOM KEP (132 C6) (*ᗡᏉ G6*)
It's possible to go on an 8 km (5 mi),
3-hour 'Jungle Trek' in this small national
park (approx. 50 sq km/20 sq mi) just
beyond Kep – it takes you up to the Sunset Rock with the most spectacular view
from the 182 m (600 ft) high Phnom Kep.
The gigantic dipterocarp trees make the
perfect playground for wild macaques.
Information: Kep Lodge and *Led Zep Café*

WAT KIRISAN (132 C6) (*ᗡᏉ G6*)
The Wat Kirisan cave temple (also known
as *Wat Kirisela/Wat Phnom*) lies in a
magical setting of steep, rugged karst ter-
rain at the foot of the wild *Phnom Sor*.
Hidden inside this partially collapsed
limestone mountain is an enchanted valley, a large reclining Buddha, as well as
hundreds of caves and passages, some of
which can be explored on all fours. *Admis-
sion approx. 5,000 KHR | about 25 km (16
mi) east of Kep near Kampong Trach (N 33)*

PHNOM PENH

▨▨ MAP INSIDE BACK COVER
(133 D4) (*ᗡᏉ H5*) **The approximately 600-year-old capital city (pop.
around 1.5 million) on the Tonle Sap
River is currently undergoing a meteoric
journey through time into the 21st century and is light years ahead of the rural
rest of the country.**
The first mirror-glassed skyscrapers in
Cambodia are already under construction here; where else! However, the city
has been able to preserve its particular
charm – a mixture of Asian (traffic) chaos,

CITY **WHERE TO START?**
Sisowath Quay (U D–E 1–3)
(*ᗡᏉ d–e 1–3)*: the promenade
along the bank of the Tonle Sap
River is the perfect starting place in
Phnom Penh; regardless of whether you want to visit the Royal Palace
and colourful markets in the south
of the city or make a night of it in
one of the many tourist bars and
restaurants on the riverbank in the
north. Walk here or have a cyclo
bring you in comfort.

typical Khmer nonchalence and French
colonial flair. A number of beautiful Art
Nouveau villas and Art Deco architectural
gems can still be seen in some districts
(along *Street 92*, for example).
Until the mid 1990s, the once-pillaged
ghost town only had seven surfaced
roads laid out in a chequered pattern;
the main boulevards changed their
names depending on whoever hap-
pened to be in power at the time – they
were once named after Marx and Lenin,
and at another time after King Sihanouk
and Charles de Gaulle.
The touristic heart of the city beats directly on the banks of the Tonle Sap on
the northern *Sisowath Quay* with its luxurious hotels and chic restaurants, cash
dispensers and travel agencies, beggars
and hawkers. The surge of Cambodian
life can be felt on the northern section of
the esplanade near the Royal Palace:
picnics, steaming cookshops, miracle
healers, ● mass aerobic gymnastics, tai
chi and badminton.
Not only are the streets and squares once
again full of life, so too are the numerous
go-go bars and monasteries. The monks are
devoted to Buddha and his teachings but
also to modern duties and diversions: such

as when they pour buckets of holy water over one of the believers' new cars or get carried away watching the World Football Championship in front to the monastery's | *daily 8am–5pm | admission 10,000 KHR | Street 13 corner of Street 178, north of the Royal Palace | www.cambodia museum.info*

The capital's tourist highlight: the lavishly decorated Silver Pagoda

TV screen. *Information: www.phnompenh. gov-kh, www.phnompenhonline.com*

SIGHTSEEING

NATIONAL MUSEUM ● (U E3) *(ℳ e3)*
The main attractions in the pagoda-like building of russet coloured brick are the most beautiful examples of art from the Angkor epoch (802–1431). Among the most precious of the 5,000, chronologically organised, exhibits are the large eight-armed *Vishnu* from the Funan era (6th century), a sandstone statue of King Jayavarman VII in the pose of the meditating Buddha (12/13th century; unfortunately without arms), the bronze sleeping *Vishnu* (11th century) and the *houseboat* of King Ang Duong, the great-grandfather of former King Sihanouk. *Photography/video only from the outside*

SILVER PAGODA (ROYAL PALACE)
★ ● (U E4) *(ℳ e4)*
The Silver Pagoda (also: *Wat Preah Keo Morokot, Temple of the Emerald Buddha*) lies in the spacious grounds of the Royal Palace that was built in 1866. Palace buildings accessible to the public include the impressive throne hall (its 59 m/194ft high spire adorned with Bayon-style faces and interior ceiling depicting scenes from the Indian Ramayana/Reamker epic) as well as several small structures on its south (left) side such as the distinctive, delicate Pavilion of Napoleon III containing the art gallery. Access to the magnificent *Silver Pagoda* itself is through a gate in the wall on the left. It was built in 1962 to replace the original wooden structure from 1892: the interior is decorated with Italian marble, silver (pay special attention to the 5,329 tiles on the floor) and

lots of gold. In the centre stands the life-size *Preah Srei Arya Métreya Buddha* (the Buddha of the Future) with upraised – signifying fearlessness – protective hands made of 90 kilograms of pure gold and adorned with 2,086 diamonds of up to 25 carats that dazzle from the head to the feet and on the hands and in the eyes of the Enlightened One. The greatly revered Emerald Buddha *(Preah Keo)* sits behind this statue atop the gilded Bossabok platform; it is a rather unprepossessing figure, about 50cm (20in) high and green in colour, probably made of baccarat crystal.

In front of the Silver Pagoda there is an *equestrian statue of King Norodom* and the *royal burial stupas*, the one on the right containing the ashes of Norodom and his wife, the parents of the long-reigning former King Sihanouk. The surrounding galleries impress with some excellently restored scenes from the Ramayana/Reamker covering around 600 sq m (6,500 sq ft); those in the eastern gallery opposite the Silver Pagoda, starting in the lower southern section, are especially admirable. *Daily 8–11am and 2–5pm | admission 20,000 KHR incl. permission to photograph (not inside the building!) and pamphlet, no admission in shorts or strap tops | Sothearos Blvd.*

TUOL SLENG GENOCIDE MUSEUM
(U C5) *(𝄞 c5)*
The Tuol Sleng Memorial Site was formerly the torture prison of the Khmer Rouge and was also known as S-21. Around 20,000 Cambodians were imprisoned and tortured here between 1975 and 1979 before being murdered on the *Killing Fields* near Choeung Ek just outside the city gates and then thrown unceremoniously into mass graves. Today, visitors to the former classrooms of a school that were converted into cells are confronted by the iron beds with handcuffs, the instruments of torture, the countless black-and-white photographs of the meticulously registered victims – many of whom were children – and the heartbreaking paintings of the inmates. A section of the building was surrounded with barbed wire to prevent suicides. Only seven prisoners managed to survive the regime of terror – they were all painters or musicians who had been forced to keep the Khmer Rouge entertained with their art. *Daily 7.30am–5.30pm; one-hour film screenings at 10am and 3pm | admission approx. 7,500 KHR | Street 113 near Street 350*

WAT PHNOM 🌿 (U D2) *(𝄞 d2)*
The approx. 30m (100ft) high temple hill of *Wat Phnom*, which is the home of countless macaque monkeys, was founded on a legend: it is said that a certain Lady Penh *(Yea Penh)* had this hill piled up in 1372 after she had found four statues of Buddha in the Mekong and needed a hallowed place in which to store them. Today, she is also venerated in the form of a statue in a shrine (the small, chubby lady with the glasses). Behind the temple with frescoes of scenes from the life of Buddha, you will see a large white stupa containing the ashes of King Ponhea Yat, the founder of Phnom Penh. Nearby, elephants stand patiently waiting to be ridden and there is also a playground. *Daily from around 7am–6pm | admission approx. 5,000 KHR | Street 19 near the river*

FOOD & DRINK

BAI THONG (U E4) *(𝄞 e4)*
Charming, small Thai restaurant, pleasantly calm, elegant and air-conditioned. In addition to Thai dishes and classics from the neighbouring countries, the

restaurant serves French cuisine and has a good selection of wines and cocktails. *Daily | 100 Sothearos Blvd, near Independence Monument | tel. 023 21 10 54 | Budget–Moderate*

BOPHA PHNOM PENH TITANIC
RESTAURANT ● (U D2) *(ᗰ d2)*

One of the most beautiful restaurants in the capital: you eat by candlelight seated in rattan chairs by the river (don't forget your mosquito repellent!) with an unbelievable choice of dishes including couscous, cheese fondue, curries, lobster and vegetarian delights. The speciality of the house: buffalo steak! Friendly service, Khmer dance show every evening 7–9pm; live band *Titanic* at weekends. *Sisowath Quay, near the ferry dock | tel. 023 42 72 09 | Budget–Moderate*

INSIDER TIP ▶ KOLAP ANGKOR
(U D4) *(ᗰ d4)*

Small, clean, informal soup kitchen with local dishes served in three sizes. Simple, rock-bottom prices and delicious; try the

beef soup *Cambodian Style* or fried noodles with seafood. *Daily | 35 B Street 55, near Independence Monument | Budget*

MALIS (U E5) *(ᗰ e5)*

Trendy, elegant garden restaurant behind a high wall (but unfortunately on a loud street) that also has air-conditioned rooms. It serves top-quality modern Khmer cuisine such as duck curry, amok and soups. Large wine cellar – a huge statue of Buddha in the courtyard oversees the quality. *Daily | 136 Street 41/ Norodom Blvd. | tel. 023 22 10 22 | Moderate–Expensive*

ONE MORE PUB (U D5) *(ᗰ d5)*

A small oasis with a lovely garden patio. German owner and chef Peter is always ready to serve his guests a cool beer, good wine and (international) home-style cooking. The house also has two simple guest rooms *(Budget)*. *Mon–Sat | 16 Eo Street 294 | tel. 017 32 73 78 | www. onemorepub.com | Moderate*

Good deeds count: daily offerings in Wat Phnom

Bargaining allowed: Art Deco shopping at the Central Market

RESTAURANT 112 (U C2) (ᵭ c2)
Fine dining in the elegant Colonial Mansion (apartments: *Expensive*). On weekdays they put on a sensationally inexpensive lunchtime buffet with tasty chicken, duck, lamb and pork dishes *(35,000 KHR); in the evening, romantic dinner* featuring signature French dishes. *The* place for a nice glass of wine. *Daily | Street 102 | tel. 023 99 08 80 | Moderate–Expensive*

THE TAMARIND (U E4) (ᵭ e4)
Popular bar-restaurant on a lovely, shady avenue. Oriental and Mexican classics, as well as pizza, pasta and Asian food are served on three floors. The ☀ roof terrace has a very special atmosphere in the evening. Extensive wine list. Happy Hour 3–7pm. *31 Street 240, to the southwest of the Silver Pagoda | tel. 012 83 01 39 | Budget*

SHOPPING

You will find many boutiques, souvenir shops, restaurants, bars and spas under shady tamarind trees on tranquil Street 240 (south of the Silver Pagoda), as well as on Street 178 with its galleries and arts-and-crafts shops.

FRIENDS@240 ☺ (U E4) (ᵭ e4)
The shop (and tailor) for a good cause: the fashionable, trendy clothes, street wear and accessories for both sexes are made by young people in the Mith Samlanh Studio; they also produce made-to-measure apparel. *Daily 10am–6.30pm | 32, Street 240, opposite Royal Palace | www.friends-international.org*

PHSAR THMAY (THMEI) (CENTRAL MARKET) (U D3) (ᵭ d3)
This gigantic ochre-yellow market has towered over the centre of Phnom Penh like a spaceship with an Art Deco covering since the 1930s. No matter whether you find it hard to make your choice between the mountains of fruit and fried tarantulas, whether you want to get the better of the jewellers under the enormous dome, or are only interested in woks, silk and

souvenirs (such as the typical ● Krama shawls), you must not forget to bargain in the four wings of the building. Just flow with the crowd through the labyrinth. *Daily, approx. 7am–5pm | at the southern end of Street 61*

PHSAR TUOL TOM PONG
(U C6) (*⑭ c6*)
The small-scale *Russian Market* can be a real goldmine. Once you have worked your way past the piles of tyres, tools and shock absorbers, you will be able to purchase all kinds of goods in a low-key atmosphere: Buddhas and apsaras of all sizes, genuine and fake antiques and branded goods, silk scarves, fine china, art-and-crafts, CDs and a great variety of bric-a-brac. *Daily 5am–5pm | Street 446 corner of Street 155 in the south of the city (east entrance)*

INSIDER TIP ► TUOL SLENG SHOES (T&T SHOES SHOP) (U C6) (*⑭ c6*)
Court shoes, slippers and sandals – nothing of top quality for the really discerning, but all made of real leather. You can buy lady's shoes from around 100,000 KHR. *Daily 7am–7pm | Street 143, near Tuol Sleng Beautiful Shows* is another family-run shoe shop in the neighbourhood.

EXCURSIONS

KHMER ARCHITECTURE TOURS ●
Cyclo tours to the buildings erected in the 1960s in a style described as 'New Khmer Architecture' (most by the famous Le-Corbusier student Vann Molyvann), including the Olympic Stadium, University, cinemas and villas (some of which are now run as boutique hotels). *Three-hour group tours in English: approx. 45,000 KHR/person; private tours: approx. 180,000 KHR / tel. 092 87 00 05 | www.ka-tours.org*

MONSOON TOURS
One of the oldest travel agencies in the country (under German management) specialises in Mekong tours (with dolphin watching, *see. p. 90*), birdwatching, as well as trips to other parts of the country. There is also an office in Siem Reap. *27 Street 351 | Sangkat Boeng Kak 1 | Tuol Kork | tel. 023 96 96 16 | www.monsoon-tours.com*

LOW BUDGET

► For as little as 20,000 KHR, you can swing in a hammock and watch the sunset at the *Kep Seaside Guesthouse* in Kep **(132 C6)** (*⑭ G6*) – also possible from some balcony rooms (number 20) Good service for next to nothing. *26 rooms | N33 to Kampot (next to Knai Bang Chatt) | tel. 012 68 42 41 | www.kep-cambodia.com/mainpages/PlacesinKep/kep-seaside.html*

► Prices for a one-hour Khmer or Thai massage (in pyjamas) or an oil massage at *Sawadee* (in the Goldie Boutique Guesthouse) **(U D5)** (*⑭ d5*) in Phnom Penh start at 30,000 KHR. *9am–11pm | Street 57 | tel. 023 99 66 70*

► *Monkey Republic* is the place in Sihanoukville **(132 B5)** (*⑭ F6*) for young travellers on a limited budget and in need of information to congregate: the bamboo bungalows in the jungle garden cost as little as 25,000 KHR (*26 rooms | tel. 012 49 02 90*) – book in good time!

SUNSET CRUISE ON THE MEKONG ★
(U D–E 2–3) (*∅ d–e 2–3*)

Everybody can have a front-row view of the sun setting in red and gold behind the Royal Palace from the sunset cruise boats on the Tonle Sap and Mekong. Regardless of whether you prefer Khmer pop music, hip-hop or something more romantic with Champagne and canapés – there is the perfect cruise for every budget. It is possible to charter an entire boat for 35,000–75,000 KHR per hour (depending on size and comfort); the boats are moored between Street 144 and Street 130, as well as at the passenger terminal near Street 104; e.g. *Kanika Katamaran (www.camentours.com)* or the beautiful pagoda-like *Raffles Boat (5–7pm | with 6 passengers; the latter costs approx. 260,000 KHR/person | Street 136 | tel. 012 84 88 02).*

ENTERTAINMENT

When you've had enough of the hustle and bustle of Sisowath Quay, you'll find many bars and restaurants on charming little Street 240. If you're looking for more action, go to the new Travellers' Corner around Streets 278 and 57 *(Boeung Keng Kang, BKK, south of the Independence Monument)* or to the bars on Streets 130, 136 and 104.

INSIDER TIP CHINESE HOUSE
(U D1) (*∅ d1*)

Lounge bar and gallery in a splendid villa built in 1904: a mix of French façade and Chinese shophouse interior – one of the few original colonial buildings left in Phnom Penh! Enjoy the relaxed atmosphere and Asian snacks and cocktails at the bar, on sofas or in the cosy corners on the veranda. *Tue–Sun from 6pm | 45 Sisowath Quay, in the north, near the container terminal | www.chinesehouse.asia*

INSIDER TIP CHOW ☼ (U E3) (*∅ e3*)

Trendy, breezy rooftop bar with a view of the nocturnal activity on the river from the sixth floor; cosy corners for chilling out and a Jacuzzi, Asian fusion snacks, happy-

The best time for a romantic cruise on the river: tropical sunset

hour beer *(6–8pm)* for an unbelievable 5,000 KHR; the 16 spacey, plush hotel rooms (*Moderate–Expensive*) are out of the ordinary but are also unfortunately overlooking noisy Sisowath Quay or have no window. *In The Quay Hotel | 277 Sisowath Quay | www.thequayhotel.com*

ELEPHANT BAR (U C2) (*m c2*)

The most famous bar in Cambodia: laid-back atmosphere with piano music or jazz and surprisingly inexpensive cocktails *(half price at happy hour 4–8pm)*. Billiards, BBQ in the garden every Thursday in the dry season, lavish seafood buffet (incl. lobster, oysters, etc. for 100,000 KHR) on Fridays. *Tue–Sun from 6pm | in Raffles Hotel Le Royal (see 'Where to Stay')*

PONTOON LOUNGE (U E3) (*m e3*)

A colourful mix of locals, expats and tourists gets together for the happy hour *(5–8pm)* or to trip the light fantastic on the river *(Sun Salsa)* on this floating dance ship. Countless cocktails, international DJs, good music mix. The vessel sank back in 2008, but the manager swears that it is now anchored so securely that even a herd of elephants could dance the pogo on it. *Sisowath Quay, at Street 108*

SHADOW PUPPET THEATRE SOUVANNA PHUM THEATRE
(U O) (*m O*)

Many artists, dancers and musicians were murdered under the Khmer Rouge regime but the old traditions come back to life every weekend here in the Souvanna Phum Theatre: shadow puppets, Khmer dance, acrobatics accompanied by the typical sounds of the *Sro lai* (Khmer flute) and the *Ro niet* (xylophone). In *Sbeik thom*, the rigid figures – some of them more than 6ft tall – usually perform tales from the Ramayana; in *Sbeik touch* smaller, moveable puppets depict scenes from everyday life (in rural areas, they are often used to inform people about the dangers of malaria and AIDS). You can also buy masks, puppets and CDs. *Fri and Sat 7.30pm | admission 17,500 KHR | 166 Street 99 | www.shadow-puppets.org*

SHARKY'S (U D3) (*m d3*)

Live concerts, air-guitar competitions, parties: there's always something happening at Sharky's – in what claims to be the 'longest running Rock 'n' Roll Bar in Indochina' (since 1995)! But, there is no denying that the drinks are well cooled, the menu is enormous (from burgers and steaks to burritos and Thai food), the music runs the gamut from funk and soul to punk (live music at the weekend), there is a mixed bunch of guests and a lot of Khmer (Viet) girls. They are not all completely 'genuine' – there are usually a few 'ladyboys' among them. *Daily from 5pm | 126 Street 130, 500m to the east of the Central Market, 1st floor | www.sharkysofcambodia.com*

WHERE TO STAY

ALMOND (U E5) (*m e5*)

Pleasant middle-class business hotel, in a peaceful location away from the hordes of tourists, with well equipped rooms (satellite TV, safe, minibar, some with balcony). *45 rooms | 128 F Sothearos Blvd in the south | tel. 023 22 08 22 | www.almondhotel.com.kh | Moderate*

INSIDER TIP BLUE LIME
(U D3–4) (*m d3–4*)

An oasis behind high walls: centrally-located boutique hotel (book in good time!) with beds and sofas in chic washed concrete (satellite TV, some rooms with balcony, room 8 has a spacious corner balcony), peaceful pool with pavilions for relaxing. *45 rooms | 42 Street 19z, lane to the west of Street 19 | tel. 023 22 22 60 | www.bluelime.asia | Moderate*

CAMBODIANA ✵ (U F4) (🗺 f4)

This classic from the 1960s has now become a bit long in the tooth. However, it still scores with its ideal location at the confluence of the Mekong and Tonle Sap, the spectacular view, pool and fitness centre. Idyllic dining pavilions over the river *(from 4pm | Budget–Moderate)*, *Qba* Nightclub with live bands *(from 8pm)*. *300 rooms | 313 Sisowath Quay | tel. 023 21 81 89 | www.hotelcambodiana. com.kh | Moderate–Expensive*

INSIDER TIP CYCLO (U D3) (🗺 d3)

Small hotel with a variety of individually furnished rooms over three floors, some with balcony (suite number 2 is split-level); the most beautiful accommodation is in the corner room number 10 (with chandelier) and number 6 with a private ✵ roof terrace! Billiards, pleasant restaurant with Belgian-French cuisine *(Budget–Moderate)*. *10 rooms | Street 172*

corner of Street 23 | tel. 023 99 21 28 | cy clo.hotel@gmail.com | Budget–Moderate*

GOLDIE BOUTIQUE GUESTHOUSE (U D5) (🗺 d5)

Informal, friendly and in the heart of the trendy *Boeung Keng Kang (BKK) travellers' district:* some rooms have balconies (satellite TV, minibar), small bathrooms, neatly decorated. *15 rooms | 6 Street 57 | tel. 023 99 66 70 | www.goldieguest house.com | Budget*

KABIKI (U E4) (🗺 e4)

This attractive guesthouse is unfortunately often full. It has small, well equipped, rooms with private gardens between dwarf palm trees, as well as a saltwater pool (many children on Sundays). The lovely *Hotel Pavilion* just around the corner in a villa dating from the 1920s is run by the same owner *(www.thepavilion. asia | Moderate)*. *11 rooms | 22 Street 264, near Wat Bodum | tel. 023 22 22 90 | www. thekabiki.com | Moderate*

RAFFLES LE ROYAL ★ (U C2) (🗺 c2)

Legendary home-away-from home for a whole string of famous guests including Somerset Maugham and Jacqueline Ken-

The 'regal' Raffles offers colonial splendour and an illustrious guest list

nedy. Book one of the Landmark Balcony Rooms in the original colonial building from 1929 where Art Deco and Khmer Deco flow into each other and the bathtubs pose regally on lions' paws. The two 25 m pools between the three (imitation) wings are a pure oasis! Special offers in the low season. *170 rooms | 92 Rukhak Vithei Daun Penh, near Wat Phnom | tel. 023 98 18 88 | phnompenh.raffles.com | Expensive*

SUNWAY (U D2) (𝄞 d2)

This 4-star hotel is popular with group travellers. Its rooms are cosily elegant; some have enormous terraces, apartments with kitchen, very good Mediterranean restaurant *(Moderate)*, and spa. *138 rooms | Street 92, at Wat Phnom | tel. 023 43 03 33 | www.sunwayhotels.com | Moderate–Expensive*

WHERE TO GO

KILLING FIELDS (CHOEUNG EK)
● (133 D4) (𝄞 H5)

This is a national memorial site and a macabre tourist attraction rolled into one. You should start your visit in the museum, which has photos of the victims and a film about the Pol Pot era (on the right as soon as you enter the site). Sometimes pieces of cloth and bones still come to the surface of the Killing Fields after heavy rains. Countless skulls with empty eye sockets staring at the visitors have been stacked up to the roof of the pagoda-like tower house. Between 1975 and 1979, the Khmer Rouge slaughtered more than 10,000 people on these Fields alone and a total of around 1.5 million Cambodians were killed during the four years of the reign of terror under Pol Pot. *Daily 8am–5pm | admission around 20,000 KHR incl. audio-guide | around 16km (10mi) to the south of Phnom Penh | www.cekillingfield.com*

Killing Fields: memories of four years of terror

SIHANOUKVILLE

(132 B5) (𝄞 F6) **In the past decade, Sihanoukville (pop. around 160,000) has developed from being a provincial harbour town to a lively seaside resort where no desire is left unfulfilled: tattoos, happy-hour cocktails, go-go bars and campfire beach parties for the travellers from the West who flock here and a casino and karaoke for Asian guests.**

The resort town (also known as *Kampong Som*; insiders simply call it *Snook*) is a multicultural stronghold for dropouts, adventurers and business people from around the world. The seven beaches on the peninsula could just as easily be on Mallorca – were it not for the women on the beach selling tempting exotic fruit from baskets suspended from their carrying poles and the hordes of Khmer tourists having fun on the beach at the weekend.

Sihanoukville boasts the greatest density of restaurants in a relatively small area, and the widest variety of Cambodian cuisine, in the country – at prices that are not even worth mentioning. The endless row of restaurants and inns at *Ochheuteal Beach* cater for their guests with candlelight seafood BBQs every evening *(around 10,000–15,000 KHR)*.

CINDERELLA CAFÉ

This relaxed, tasteful café is run by Rainer from Stuttgart who attaches great importance to 😊 reusable straws and bamboo spoons: goulash, salads and spaghetti, top-quality Lavazza coffee and cocktails. Occasional evening concerts with guitar and flute music. There are twelve attractive guestrooms *(Cinderella Golden Lodge | Budget–Moderate)*, and the owner also has INSIDER TIP six spartan huts (generator electricity 6–11pm) for rent on the delightfully secluded *Otres Beach (around 5km/3mi from Sihanoukville | Budget)*. *Daily | Serendipity Beach Road, 50m from the Lion Monument on the roundabout | tel. (restaurant) 092 61 20 35 | www.cinderella-cambodia.com | Budget–Moderate*

MARCO POLO

This restaurant serves the best salads, pasta, *pizza e vino*, and other Italian classics in its garden and on the veranda. *Daily | on the road to Sokha Beach, around 100m to the west of the Lion Statue on the roundabout | tel. 092 92 08 66 | Budget–Moderate*

TREASURE ISLAND

This idyllic seafood restaurant on the beach at the extreme western tip mainly attracts local guests to its pavilions and tables in the sand. They order delicious squid in black pepper sauce, shrimp soup, fried noodles and steaks – all 'Hong Kong style' and served in three different sizes. Don't forget your mosquito protection! *Daily | road between Independence Beach and Hawaii Beach | tel. 012 83 05 05 | Budget*

SNAKE HOUSE

Novel restaurant with mini-zoo and crocodile farm *(admission 10,000 KHR for people who do not eat in the restaurant)*,

The international traveller community's stomping ground: Ochheuteal Beach

where international and Russian specialities are served surrounded by crocs, poisonous snakes, geckos, spiders and other creatures (don't worry: they are all in terrariums). Also a few bungalows *(Budget–Moderate). Daily | above Victory Beach on the hill of the same name | tel. 012 67 38 05 | Budget*

SPORTS & ACTIVITIES

ISLAND HOPPING

(132 B5–6) (*⑩ E–F6*)

Popular day trips take visitors to *Koh Russei (Bamboo Island, 45 min)*, which has now become overrun with tourists who are lackadaisically served picnic style food in front of the toilets on the not-so-clean 200 m beach (there are ten overpriced huts of the simplest kind with squat toilets, electricity 6–11pm, *Budget*). You'll have to travel further to reach *Koh Dek Koul* (a tiny island with a kitschy, super-luxurious Russian resort, *www.miraxresort.com | Expensive)* and INSIDER TIP *Koh Rong Samloem (around 2 hours)* with several secluded beaches, a lighthouse and simple bungalow complexes *(www.lazybeachcambodia.com, www.ecosea*

dive.com and www.kohrongsamloem. com (M´Pay Bay Bungalows) | all Budget), and remote *Koh Tan (4–5 hours)* where only soldiers live. There are other spartan huts for hippie Robinson Crusoes on *Koh Rong*, the new dream beach everybody wants to visit these days *(2 hours by boat; not to be confused with Koh Rong Samloem)*. There, you can loll around in your hammock and watch the sun disappear below the horizon. *The boat tours cost from around 30,000 KHR per person depending on the distance*

If you'd prefer to go ● island hopping in more style (and with more safety), you should hop aboard Sun Tours, a three-deck excursion boat with sundeck and seven double cabins and Robert the chef waiting to pamper his guests. There are also dinner cruises and fishing and diving tours lasting several days. *Day trip to Koh Rong Samloem approx. 105,000 KHR/person | www.suntours-cambodia.com,* or through *Local Adventures in Phnom Penh: tel. 023 990460.*

INSIDER TIP ► KOH TA KIEV

(132 B5) (*⑩ F6*)

While everybody flocks to Bamboo Island on their super-cheap day trip, the Koh Ta Kiev Resort, with its 1 km long, narrow sandy beach under palm and casuarina trees on the island opposite, remains almost deserted. Robinson Crusoes can live in simple, bamboo stilt huts that have been decorated with care with hammocks and floor cushions on the veranda. Terrace restaurants with typical local dishes *(Budget)*. Kayaking, sauna, fishing *5 rooms | closed in the rainy season | tel. 011 70 87 95 and 068 33 38 87.*

An even more adventurous alternative for the intrepid is Ten 103 Treehouse Bay (formerly, Jonty's Jungle camp): army hammocks with mosquito nets and rain cover. Don't forget to take along your headlamp, a death-dealing mosquito spray and ear plugs to block out the din the animals make at night. Three open tree-houses are hidden in the thicket but the real hit is the eucalyptus steam sauna next to the solar-operated toilets and showers *(Koh Ta Kiev | tel. 017 66 20 15 or through Matthew in the Ocean Walk Inn in Sihanoukville | www.ten103.com | Budget)*.

By the way, Koh Ta Kiev has been leased to French-Malayan investors and that means that we will soon see gigantic 'environmentally friendly' hotels with a marina and golf course. Robinson had better get a move on...

DIVING

The Dive Shop Cambodia organises dive courses, scuba trips and snorkelling excursions to 25 different dive sites and islands, open-water Padi courses and night dives under German-Turkish supervision, best time: Nov–March. *On the road to Serendipity Beach, next to Monkey Republic | tel. 034 93 36 63 and 034 93 36 64 | www.diveshopcambodia.com*

BEACHES

You have a choice of seven different beaches (from the north to the south):

BOOKS & FILMS

▶ **The Road of Lost Innocence** – In this book, Somaly Mam describes her way out of child prostitution and her struggle against the sex mafia as the President of the 'Afesip' Organisation

▶ **In the Shadow of the Banyan** – Moving autobiographical novel by Vaddey Ratner about a young girl's desperate battle for survival under the Khmer Rouge.

▶ **Same Same but different** – This 2009 film, based on Benjamin Prüfers book 'Wohin Du auch gehst' describes his 'almost impossible love' for the young HIV-positive prostitute Sreykeo and his affectionate, but exasperated, observations of Cambodia (with David Kross; directed by Detlev Buck)

▶ **The Killing Fields** – This film describes the final days before the fall of Phnom Penh to the Khmer Rouge from the viewpoint of the American journalist Sidney Schanberg and his assistant Dith Pran – it won three Oscars and was John Malkovich's debut film (USA 1984; directed by: Roland Joffé)

▶ **City of Ghosts** – The Bokor National Park, with its eerie atmosphere, provided the setting for this sinister, brutal thriller with Matt Dillon, James Caan and Gérard Depardieu (USA 2002; directed by Matt Dillon). By the way, truth became stranger than fiction in a typically Cambodian way when, in 2006, two security officers actually died at a party in the Bokor Casino.

▶ **Tomb Raider** – Several key scenes in this action film, with Angelina Jolie in the role of the fantastic Lara Croft (USA 2001; directed by Simon West), were shot in the Ta Prohm temple ruins

VICTORY BEACH AND HAWAII BEACH

Two small sunset beaches that are not very attractive due to being located close to the harbour and hotel construction projects – more for the locals.

INDEPENDENCE BEACH AND SOKHA BEACH

Occupied – and partially closed off – by the two luxury hotels with the same names, each one is about 1 km long, nice and wide and almost deserted, with casuarina trees providing the shade; you might even see some lone Zebu oxen trotting across the slightly rocky Independence Beach. *Both about 1km away.*

SERENDIPITY BEACH AND OCHHEUTEAL BEACH

The two beaches are connected and together they're about 5km (3mi) long. This is the place to come if you happen to be looking for holiday fun and games with seafood restaurants and volleyball matches, sunshades and wooden sunbeds, hawkers, manicurists and masseuses, (organised) begging children, banana boats and jetskis. The only bungalows directly on the sand are at Serendipity Beach.

OTRES BEACH

Approximately 3 km (2 mi) long beach, shaded by casuarinas, that until mid-2010 had very simple corrugated-iron dormitories and environmentally friendly accommodation. They were then either evacuated or demolished and only one or two resorts remain including the Cinderella Bungalows we mentioned before. *About 3km (2mi) southeast of Sihanoukville.*

ENTERTAINMENT

AIRPORT

All you have to do is slap an out-of-service Antonov on top of a truck and build a hall around it to get the original, way-out Airport Disco (techno, house) with its restaurant (*Budget*) and Beach Bar. *Daily from 9pm | Victory Beach*

Heavenly solitude on Sokha Beach

TOP CAT CINEMA ●

This cinema often shows demanding films and documentaries (such as *Killing Fields*) that you can watch in air-conditioned comfort in plush seats, with ice cream, popcorn and Dolby Surround. There is also an open-air cinema on the road up Victory Hill. *Daily 4–10pm, several shows | 10,000 KHR | on the road to Serendipity Beach, opposite Monkey Republic*

WHERE TO STAY

INSIDER TIP ▶ COOLABAH RESORT

Chic, modern rooms (satellite TV, safe, minibar), all spick and span; the glass squat showers are a real hit. *11 rooms | on the road to Ochheuteal Beach, approx. 300m from the beach | tel. 017 67 82 18 | www.coolabah-hotel.com | Moderate*

INDEPENDENCE HOTEL ☆
Magnificently restored, secluded, beach hotel: once a meeting place for the jet set, the high-rise hotel now offers its guests seven floors of elegant rooms with every comfort, pool and spectacular view. You should at least take a peek inside the ● lobby. Secluded Sunset Bar on the private beach; great discounts (40 percent!) in the off-season. *52 rooms | Independence Beach | tel. 034 93 43 00 | www.independencehotel.net | Expensive*

NEW SEA VIEW VILLA & RESTAURANT
Very beautiful, bright, lovingly decorated rooms – some of them are extremely spacious – with good mattresses. Massages available, and the lively restaurant has a fabulous selection of tasty dishes as well as countless cakes, ice cream and other sweet things *(Sun closed | Budget)*. *15 rooms | on the road to Serendipity Beach, approx. 50m from the beach | mobile tel. 092 75 97 53 | www.sihanoukville-hotel.com | Budget–Moderate*

REEF RESORT
Comfortable rooms with balconies on two floors around the pool in the peaceful courtyard (satellite TV, DVD, safe, minibar). Mexican restaurant *(Moderate)* with 37 different brands of tequila! *14 rooms | on the road to Serendipity Beach, approx. 500m from the beach | tel. 034 93 42 81 | www.reefresort.com.kh | Moderate*

WHERE TO GO

INSIDER TIP ▶ KOH KONG
(132 A4) (*Ø E5*)
After the completion of the N48, the city of Koh Kong (also known as *Dong Tong*; pop. approx. 50,000; 220km/136mi northwest of Sihanoukville) on the Koh Poi River metamorphosed from being just another spot on the road to Thailand just 10km (6mi) away to an escape for people who found Sihanoukville too hectic. It has potential for eco-tourism that has so far not really been exploited: Koh Kong is surrounded by mangroves, rivers and beaches that are still intact to a large extent; in the distance the wild *Cardamom Mountains* soar up into the sky; up to 1,800m (5,900ft) high, they are a kind of Cambodian Jurassic Park with what is claimed to be the second-largest area of jungle on the Southeast Asian mainland after Myanmar.

In the vicinity are some attractive waterfalls such as the 5 m (16ft) high *Ta Tai* (20km/12mi to the east), the *Ko Por* and *Kbal Chhay*. Excursions to the island of the same name (*Koh Kong*, the largest island in the country, but one that is almost totally uninhabited), eco-trekking and jeep tours into the mountains, as well as boat trips to the *Peam Krasaop Wildlife Sanctuary*, promise some extraordinary adventures in the deserted wilderness.

The *4 Rivers Floating Eco Lodge* is something unique, especially for those seeking peace and quiet: it's more like a luxurious, floating tent hideaway on a river in the middle of the jungle. You can leap straight into the water from the terrace, take excursions into the surroundings, go kayaking and relax in the spa but, apart from that, there is not much to do... Not really recommendable in the rainy season. *(12 rooms | Peam Krasaop, boat transfer at 2 and 5pm from the village of Tatai | tel. in Phnom Penh 023 21 73 74 | www.ecolodges.asia | Expensive).*

The *casino* and *Safari World Zoo* on the border are more appealing to pleasure seekers (Thais, mainly). The small *Oasis* on the northern edge of town delivers what it promises: simple, bungalows suitable for families (satellite TV, refrigerator) with verandas facing the pool (5 rooms | Smach Mean Chey | tel. 092 22 83 42 | oasisresort.netkhmer.com | *Budget)*. The rustic *Baracuda Beach Bar* and the attached PADI Diving School take care of their guests with seafood, fruit shakes ands ice-cold beer *(Koh Yor Beach | tel. 017 50 27 84 | Budget)*. Otto's is famous all over Koh Kong City *(www. koh-kong.com | Budget)*.

REAM NATIONAL PARK

(132 B5) *(ɯ F6)*

Trekking and boat tours on the Preak Reak River in the Ream National Park (also known as: *Preah Sihanouk*; 210 sq km/81 sq mi) take visitors into the jungle and the *Andoung Tuek Waterfall*, through ecologically-important mangrove swamps with their feathered inhabitants (such as the fish eagle, storks and kingfishers), and to beaches and fishing villages. It is also possible to head out to sea on snorkelling tours to the dolphins and the distant *Koh Thmei* and *Koh Ses islands* (around 3 hours away). *7am–5pm | 18km (11mi) east of Sihanoukville on the N 4 | National Park Office with English-speaking rangers | tel. 012 87 50 96 | four-hour boat charter ap-*prox. 165,000 KHR, *organised half-day tour departing from Sihanoukville 40,000–75,000 KHR/person (depending on number of participants); two-hour dolphin tours approx. 75,000 KHR/person, 7–9am and 3.30–5pm, Nov–March*

It is possible to spend the night in basic huts near the *Dolphin Station (Budget)* or in INSIDERTIP *Koh Thmei Resort (7 rooms | 60 min by boat from Koh Kchhang village to Koh Thmei | mobile tel. 097 7 37 04 00 and 089 89 78 30 | www. koh-thmei-resort.com | Budget)* in rustic environmentally-friendly, stilt huts on the long shell beach with the offshore coral reef. You will live very simply if you stay with the German emigrants Kavita and Michael but will receive a warm welcome, almost as if you were part of the family, in the only resort on the island, equipped with solar electricity, torches, mosquito nets, hammocks on the terrace, coldwater showers and ceiling fans. You can take excursions to other parts of the 40 sq km (15 sq mi) island and watch rare birds and bats; the restaurant mainly serves Khmer dishes, seafood and a few local snacks and cake from time to time.

Ream National Park: the people living in stilt houses on the Preak Reak River have a simple lifestyle

ANGKOR & SIEM REAP

Over 1,000 years ago, the Khmer kings (802–1431) ruled more than 1 million subjects and the major part of Southeast Asia. After the fall of the 'god kings', the jungle gradually swallowed up the buildings that are among the most magnificent artistic masterpieces and architectural miracles of Asia, if not the world. Although the royal city of Angkor is one of UNESCO's World Heritage Sites, it is anything but a museum. Around 30,000 people live and work in the complex; joss sticks and small offerings lie in front of the statues of Buddha. Wedding groups take up their poses in front of Angkor Wat, the largest religious building on earth: the Khmer bride in her glittering gold dress, with a small crown in her hair adorned with hibiscus blossoms, could be a prin-

cess from the realm of King Jayarvarman VII come back to life – if she wasn't wearing heavy platform-soled shoes.

The rapid increase in the number of tourists has transformed Siem Reap, 6km (4mi) away, from a sleepy market town into a bustling tourist centre where visitors to Angkor will now find a fully developed infrastructure with hotels and restaurants. It is difficult to imagine now, but the nearby Phnom Kulen mountains and the little visited region around Battambang were once the stronghold of the Khmer Rouge. Violent battles were even taking place here as recently as 1993–5, following the withdrawal of the UN troops. Boat tours now take visitors across the seemingly endless Tonle Sap Lake with its houseboat settlements and

Photo: Ta Prohm Temple

The legendary ruined city of Angkor is the symbol of Cambodia – and the villages float on Tonle Sap Lake

stilt houses. These trips end in Battambang, the charming, second-largest city in Cambodia.

ANGKOR

DETAILED MAP ON PAGE 134
(128 C3) (*F2*) **The column of buses and tuktuks sets out from Siem Reap along the 6 km (4 mi) long road towards Angkor in the early hours of the morning, in order to be there in time for the sunrise. The silhouettes of the towers of Angkor Wat etched like cut outs against the dawn sky are something everybody wants to experience.**

The 800-year-old main building of the ruined city, with its five striking spires, depicts Mount Meru – the seat of the gods from the Hindu pantheon. The monotonous chanting of the monks reciting the *dharma*, Buddha's teachings, can be heard emanating from neighbouring monastery. There were once 600 temples dotted around the historical city of Angkor, which covered a vast area of around 1,000 sq km (400 sq mi) – around two-thirds the size of Greater London! Today, around 100 temple ruins survive. The main ones, in addition to the famous *Angkor Wat* monastery, include: *Angkor Thom* with massive stone faces adorning the towers of the Bayon; the *ruins of Ta*

6pm at the latest, when the temples are closed). The entrance fee for one day is around 70,000 KHR (you'll need a passport photo, which can be taken on the spot), for three days around 140,000 KHR (valid for one week), or for seven days 210,000 KHR (valid for one month). If you buy a ticket after 5pm, you can im-

Novice monks in front of old ruins – Buddhism is alive and well in Cambodia

Prohm, which are firmly in the clutches of the mammoth roots of gigantic jungle trees; and the enchanting *devatas* (in everyday language: *apsaras*) in *Banteay Srei*. The complex's countless sandstone sculptures and reliefs depict the history of Vishnu, the Hindu god and protector of the world, and scenes from everyday Khmer life. The dancing apsaras, the mythical garuda birds, the monkeys and demons provide eternal proof of the former advanced civilisation of the Khmer.

Tickets for the temple complex are available from the ticket booths *(5am–5.30pm)* of the *Angkor Archaeological Park*. Most temples lie between 6–12km (4–8mi) north of Siem Reap and are open daily from 5.30am to sunset (or

mediately follow the masses rushing to see the sunset in the temple complex without cancelling it. Guides charge 75,000–100,000 KHR a day *(www.guideangkor.com)*.

Two circular routes lead visitors past the buildings: the *Petit Circuit* (17km/11mi) and the *Grand Circuit* (26km/16 miles). The best way to cover these tours is with a three day ticket using taxis *(around 75,000–90,000 KHR/day)*, tuktuks *(around 35,000–55,000 KHR/day)*, moped-taxis *(around 25,000–35,000 KHR/day)* or bicycles *(around 7,500 KHR/day | www.thewhitebicycles.org, donate their income to the needy and social projects)*, some with electric motor *(around 15,000 KHR/day)* – your hotel will be able to reserve one of these vehicles for you in no time. It is also possible to take an elephant ride near the Bayon Temple *(half hour: approx. 35,000 KHR)* or to *Phnom Bakheng* for the ever-popular sunset *(approx. 60,000 KHR, in baskets on the elephant's back, reserve in good time!)*.

Thousands of hobby photographers flock to the most popular places for pictures of the sunrise *(5.30–6.30am in front of Angkor Wat)* and sunset *(around 5.30/6.30pm on ☀ Phnom Bakheng and ☀ Angkor Wat)* and between November and March in particular they tend to be hopelessly overcrowded. But there are more peaceful alternatives, such as very early morning at the *Bayon* (when the mysterious faces gradually appear in the sunlight) or the *Ta Prohm* and ☀ *Phnom Bakheng*; for the late afternoon and at sunset, options include ☀ *Phnom Bok (25km/16 miles east of Siem Reap)* or the ☀ *Phnom Krom (12km/7mi south of Siem Reap on Tonle Sap Lake, p. 82)*, as well as the ☀ temple mountain *Pre Rup (8km/5mi northeast of Angkor Wat)* or the ancient royal swimming pool *Sras Srang (6km/4mi northeast of Angkor Wat near Ta Prohm)*. There are hardly any tour groups in the temples at lunchtime and in the rainy months September and October. Those who are fascinated by temples smothered in tree roots, Indiana Jones-style, should visit *Banteay Kdei (12th/13th century)* and *Ta Som (12th century)* in addition to Ta Prohm in the Archaeological Park. The temples outside Angkor, *Beng Mealea (60km/37mi to the east | admission 20,000 KHR)* and *Koh Ker (40,000 KHR | see p. 102)* are hardly visited and still overgrown.

By the way: If a monk or temple servant gives you some joss sticks to pray with in front of a statue of Buddha, you should either refuse – but with a friendly smile – or bow three times in front of the shrine with the burning sticks in your hand; and, of course, donate a few riels.

SIGHTSEEING

ANGKOR THOM (BAYON) ★

DETAILED MAP ON PAGE 135

Five gates lead into Angkor Thom, the city of Jayavarman VII (1181 to c. 1220). Covering an area of 9 sq km (3.5 sq mi), it was larger than any city in Europe at the time and would have governed a population of around a million people in the surrounding area. A bridge leads to the south gate, which is very popular with visitors *(a little over 1 mile north of Angkor Wat)*, flanked as it is by 54 gods and 54 demons, each with a Naga serpent in its arms 'churning the sea of milk' (see Angkor Wat). Four monumental faces on the tower above the gate look to the north, south, east and west. The immense Buddhist sanctuary of Bayon rises up on three terraces in the centre of the ancient city; 37 of its former 54 towers have been preserved, as have around 200 gigantic stone, enigmatically smiling, faces that appear not to let visitors out of their sight for a moment. This

Gods and demons stand guard in front of the south gate of the gigantic city of Angkor Thom

is not at all surprising – they are representations of Lokeshvara (also: Avalokiteschvara), a Bodhisattva who, in Mahayana Buddhism, helps the faithful on their path towards Nirvana while rejecting the last stage of enlightenment himself.

Surrounding the temple are two galleries bearing an extraordinary collection of bas-reliefs depicting scenes of everyday life in Angkor, such as markets, the circus and musicians, men at cockfights, etc, as well as historical and mythological subjects. The third level of the central tower is encircled by a labyrinth of corridors with small dark chambers where bald, white-robed nuns sit in prayer and joss sticks glow in the gloom. The most peaceful time here is early in the morning at sunrise and then again in the later afternoon after 4 or 5pm; the other times are better for taking photographs. A pleasant, partly shaded, walk takes you from the Bayon to the *Baphuon,* around 200m to the north, and the following ruins. Udayadityavarman II had the Baphuon erected around 1060, but the five-level, pyramidal temple and mountain of the gods collapsed shortly after it was completed thanks to structural defects. The ruins have remained an enormous puzzle with thousands of blocks of rock and sandstone that French archaeologists have been trying to put back together since 1908 and, once again since 1995 with the use of computer software: e.g. the two platforms *(admission 6am–3pm)* and the relief of an almost 70 m (230 ft) long Buddha on the west façade that was not completely restored until 2008. Stroll further along the 350 m (1,150ft) long *Elephant Terrace,* a 2.5 m (8 ft) high platform for Jayavarman VII with parades of elephants, garuda birds and lions – immortalised as life-size reliefs on the base. Rising up behind (to the west) are the remains of the multi-storeyed *Palace*

of Heaven (Phimeanakas), including swimming pools for the concubines and men. A few steps further on, you will reach the 25 m (82 ft) long Terrace of the Leprosy King, probably named after the statue that can be seen there showing either King Yasovarman I, who died of leprosy, or the god of death Yama (the original is in the National Museum in Phnom Penh). Pay particular attention to the wonderfully preserved INSIDER TIP bas-reliefs from the 13th century hidden below the terrace on the southern inside wall: they depict heavenly apsara dancers, demons and nagas.

ANGKOR WAT ★ ●
DETAILED MAP ON PAGE 134

King Suryavarman II (c. 1112–50), who worshiped Vishnu as the supreme god, had this majestic structure built – probably as a state temple – in the first half of the 12th century; it later served as a tomb. The king, priests and officials, as well as servants, were the only ones allowed to enter Angkor Wat – probably around 20,000 people in all. With its perfect geometry, the partially restored monastery symbolises Meru, the mountain of the gods, and the Hindu universe which every visitor traverses after going through the entrance portal: first the sandstone bridge over the 190 m (620 ft) wide moat (the 'primeval sea'), then the almost 500 m (1,640 ft) long causeway with the seven-headed naga serpents as a symbolic bridge leading the 'mortal' visitors into the sanctuary.

At the end of the causeway is the cruciform terrace, or platform, which provides a transition into the divine realm of the temple itself. The galleries surrounding the base of the temple have total length of 800m, forming the world's longest series of bas-reliefs. Walk (to the right) past scenes of everyday life in Angkor and from the world of the Indian Rama-yana/Reamker and Mahabharata legends: entire hosts of legendary monkey creatures, of generals and soldiers, elephants and chariots in historical battles. Suryavarman II can be made out in the middle of the next gallery (south side), shaded by 15 umbrellas as a sign of his rank. Go around the corner and you will find yourself in the eastern gallery and in front of the most famous relief: the gods and demons 'Churning of the Sea of Milk'– they twist and turn the almost endless naga serpent Vasuki around to release the essence of immortality, the *amrita*. Also taking part: monkey-general Hanuman, Indra the god of war, a five-headed Shiva, and Vishnu in his incarnation as a giant tortoise. On your way back round towards the starting point, the galleries on the western side feature the most famous Ramayana story, the Battle of Lanka: sitting on Hanuman's shoulders, Rama fights against the ten-headed demon king Ravana who had abducted Rama's bride Sita.

Via inner courtyards and hair-raisingly steep steps leading up to a height of 42m (138ft), with breath-taking panoramic views on all sides, visitors reach the temple's geometric centre: the 60 m (213 ft) high ✳ central tower in the form of a lotus bud. Today, the dwelling of the gods – once with a gilded statue of Vishnu – is the home of a statue of Buddha. Around 1,850 bas-relief images have been counted in Angkor Wat alone. *Approx. 6km (4mi) north of Siem Reap; you should definitely visit the site at different times of the day: the most peaceful periods are before 7.30am and between 10.30am and 3pm (covered galleries), the best light is in the afternoon and the ideal place for photographing the sunrise is at the northern pool, though you won't be alone*

PHNOM BAKHENG (128 C3) (*m F2*)

Sunset wouldn't be sunset in Angkor without the Phnom Bakheng *(1.3km northwest of Angkor Wat, 400m to the south of the south gate of Angkor Thom)*: thousands of hobby photographers flock to the 67 m (220 ft) high temple mountain (erected under Yasovarman I, 889–910) in the late afternoon. It could also be described as the regular evening 'sunset battle' – as a matter of fact, in 1994, you could actually still meet soldiers with their weapons at the ready here.

The magnificent view of Angkor Wat, the rice fields, lakes and mountains from Angkor's first ✳ temple mountain more than makes up for the steep, 15-minute climb, which of course can be done at other times of day as well (e.g. from sunrise to 11am). The temple ruins rise up over five levels, with a staircase flanked by guardian lions leading to the top. It is possible to take an elephant ride up to the base of the temple if you book in good time *(ca. 60,000–90,000 KHR)*.

PREAH KHAN (128 C3) (*m G2*)

This rambling temple *(c. 1 mile north-east of the north gate of Angkor Thom, approx. 8km/5mi north of Angkor Wat)*, which was completed in the reign of Jayavarman VII in 1191, impresses visitors with its towers, corridors and archways, the 72 gigantic sandstone garudas standing guard and the slender, elegant apsaras. This large sanctuary was dedicated to a total of 515 Hindu and Buddhist deities and was also the site of religious celebrations and ancestral worship. In addition, it functioned as a monastery school and ancient clinic and as the residence of the king for a period while Angkor Thom was being built. The almost-Greek appearance of the two-storey pavilion with the round columns, which are unusual for Angkor, near the eastern entrance, will come as a surprise. It is possible that this is where the holy royal sword, which gave the temple its name, was stored. A beautiful INSIDER TIP subject for photographers near the east gate (at the back) is the strangler fig tree, its roots clasped onto the walls and roof. Best time to visit: noon to 2pm.

The *Visitor Center* of the World Monument Fund *(www.wmf.org)* near the main western entrance provides a good summary of the restoration work carried out since 1991 including a first-rate reconstruction of the 'House of Fire' rest house.

The most picturesque and photogenic of all the ruins in the rampant jungle: Ta Prohm

TA KEO (128 C3) *(G2)*

Construction of this temple mountain *(c. 6km/4mi northeast of Angkor Wat)* was begun by Jayavarman V at the end of the 10th century and probably never completed (the five massive Prasat towers lack any decorative masonry art). The sanctuary was built in honour of Shiva as can be recognised by the kneeling bull Nandi – the animal he rode on – at the entrance and the phallic *lingas* symbolising the Hindu god in the towers. The top can be reached via a narrow flight of high steps.

TA PROHM ★ (128 C3) *(G2)*

Overgrown, burst apart and simultaneously held together by the roots of the gigantic kapok trees and strangler figs, you will experience something of an enchanted atmosphere between the piles of rubble, towers and lop-sided lintels in Ta Promh. A conscious decision was made not to restore the monastery built by Jayavarman VII in 1186 *(c. 6km/4 miles northeast of Angkor Wat)*, with the exception of the wooden footbridges, and this has made it one of the most fascinating sites in Angkor with a very special quality that makes one realise that nothing lasts forever. Here, you will be able to feel like Henri Mouhout, one of the first (re)discoverers of Angkor, or like Angelina Jolie in the action film 'Tomb Raider' – one of the key scenes was shot here in the year 2000. Hollywood had its Lara Croft parachute down to Phnom Bakheng and be blessed by real monks, dive over (polystyrene) balustrades in Ta Prohm, and even fire off a rocket launcher in front of the ruins. You should try to visit the complex between the tourist

ful and peaceful in the early morning from sunrise to around 7.30am, and from 1 to 2.30pm in the afternoon.

FOOD & DRINK

There are snack bars and souvenir shops in front of all the famous temples. A recommended restaurant is *Chez Sophea & Matthieu (Moderate–Expensive)* outside

Things have a meditative, tranquil pace here: Banteay Kdei lies off the beaten track

groups (the **INSIDER TIP** Banteay Kdei monastery ruins from the 12/13th century not far away to southeast are a similarly fascinating alternative, or you can listen to the handicapped Khmer musicians playing their instruments at the entrance).

Ta Prohm is a Buddhist flat temple surrounded by moats and four-sided galleries. Seeing the labyrinthine chaos of stone blocks in the courtyard, it is almost impossible to believe that around 12,000 people, including many monks, once lived at this university. *Especially beauti-*

Angkor Wat. It is a little less expensive to eat in the *Cafe d'Angkor (outside Angkor Wat | Budget)* and *Eat at Khmer (outside Angkor Wat and Sras Srang | Budget)*.

TOURS

INSIDER TIP HANUMAN TOURISM
How about going on a completely different kind of safari? You can spend the night in comfortable bush tents near the more remote temples (e.g. *Preah Vihear*, p. 67, *Koh Ker*, p. 102/Tour 2). The 'Temple Safaris' are offered by one of the

oldest travel agencies in Cambodia. *12 Street 310 | Phnom Penh | tel. 023 21 83 96 | www.hanumantourism.com*

SIGHTSEEING

HELICOPTER FLIGHTS ★

You should try to get a bird's-eye view of the vast expanse of the temple complex: an 8-minute flight (only Angkor Wat) costs approx. 330,000 KHR; 14 min, 550,000 KHR; there are also considerably more expensive flights to the more distant temples such as Preah Vihear. *658 Hup Guan St. | Siem Reap | tel. 063 96 33 16 | www.helicopterscambodia.com*

WHERE TO GO

BANTEAY SREI ★ (129 D3) (*⑪ F2*)

This small temple, which was only discovered by French scientists in 1914, has some of the most impressive stonemasonry in Angkor and is now overrun with tourists – some areas have had to be closed off in order to protect the masterpiece. The sanctuary was constructed of red sandstone (10th century) and charms visitors with its absolutely perfect, magical reliefs that appear almost three-dimensional – above all, the devatas, the amazingly beautiful goddesses in the tower niches that seem to follow the visitors' every move with their glances. You should also look how the many-armed demon king Ravana shakes Mount Kailash, where Shiva and Uma sit enthroned, above the entrance to the southern *library*. Try if you can to visit the temple before 7am (the tour buses start arriving at 7.30am), in the early afternoon (the best light is at around 2pm) or later (4pm). *(Daily 5am–5pm | 25km/16mi northeast of Angkor, 35km/22mi from Siem Reap)*. The visit can be combined with the following sites

ON APSARAS, LINGAS AND NAGAS

▶ **apsaras** – heavenly, nymph-like dancers; often in groups of three on reliefs
▶ **Bodhisattva** – 'Enlightened existence' that renounces nirvana to assist humans on their quest towards it
▶ **devarajas** – the 'god-kings' who founded the Khmer Empire
▶ **dharma** – the teachings of Buddha
▶ **devatas** – goddesses, often opulently adorned, female guards standing upright
▶ **gopura** – tower-like gate or pavilion at the entrance to a temple
▶ **karma** – the law of destiny according to which good actions during one's lifetime decide one's fate in the next
▶ **linga** – phallic symbol of Shiva

▶ **Lokeshvara (Avalokiteshvara)** – 'Lord of the World', a Bodhisattva
▶ **nagas** – ancient deities in the form of serpents and dragons, creators of the Mekong and many Asian kingdoms. The Naga King has the form of a many-headed cobra; often at the end of a staircase or balustrade
▶ **nirvana** – the 'extinction' of the existence at the end of the cycle of rebirth (and suffering), attainable through enlightenment
▶ **phnom** – mountain, hill
▶ **prasat** – temple tower
▶ **sanskrit** – ancient Indian language
▶ **stung, tonle** – river, lake
▶ **wat** – Buddhist monastery

to make a day's excursion: *Kbal Spean (12km/7mi northwest)*, *Phnom Kulen* and, if time permits, the *Mine Museum* and possibly *Beng Mealea* if you set out very early.

BANTEAY SREY BUTTERFLY FARM ☺
(129 D3) (*ω F2*)

If you're looking for a colourful change of pace, this is the right place, especially if you have children with you: thousands of butterflies native to Cambodia flutter around a tropical garden under a net. The place is a photographer's dream, with one specimen more beautiful than the next. The guides explain the lifecycle: from the caterpillars that are bred on special farms in the region and then exported, to pupation and the boiling of the cocoons (to unravel the thread for making silk) to the moment when the hovering beauties emerge. The project supports surrounding communities and caterpillar farms. *Daily 9am–5pm | entrance fee: adults 15,000 KHR, children 7,500 KHR | 25km/16mi north of Siem Reap, on the road to Banteay Srei | www.angkorbutterfly.com*

AKI RA'S MINE MUSEUM (CAMBODIA LAND MINE MUSEUM RELIEF FACILITY) (128–129 C–D3) (*ω G2*)

The founder of this museum, Aki Ra, spent years as a serviceman defusing mines that he himself had laid as child soldier of the Khmer Rouge. The complex also has a kind of training minefield that you can cross with a detector, an informative exhibition with many deactivated mines, grenades and other weapons, a school and a ☺ rehabilitation centre for mine victims. This is not to be confused with the purely commercial mine museum on the N6! *Daily 7am–6pm | entrance fee approx. 5,000 KHR | northeast of Siem Reap on the Angkor grounds, ap-* prox. 6km (4mi) south of Banteay Srei | www.cambodialandminemuseum.org

PHNOM KULEN AND KBAL SPEAN (RIVER OF THE THOUSAND LINGAS)
★ (129 D3) (*ω G2*)

The 487 m (1,598 ft) high sacred mountain of Phnom Kulen in the national park of the same name is considered the birthplace of the Khmer empire. In 802AD, Jayarvarman II had himself crowned here as the first *devaraja* ('god-king') and founded his empire Mahendraparvata which shortly thereafter moved to Roluos. *Wat Preah Ang Thom* at the ☖ summit, which has magnificent views over the surrounding countryside, is very popular with Khmer visitors, especially at weekends. They leave their offerings at an 8 m (26 ft) long statue of the reclining Buddha reaching nirvana, before going to the nearby 30 m (100 ft) high waterfall for a picnic.

The *Kbal Spean* (also known as: *River of the Thousand Lingas*) lies hidden deep in the rainforest on the western fringes of the gigantic Phnom Kulen Plateau and was only discovered by a French scientist in 1969. The river has flowed over countless reliefs chiselled from the rock for thousands of years. They show scenes from the Ramayana, reclining Vishnu, Brahma and Shiva, apsaras and hundreds of small lingas, the phallic fertility symbols that symbolise Shiva and supposedly make the river's water more fecund for irrigating the rice fields. You should stay on the slightly sloping path *(1.5km, approx. 45 min)* because the area was a battle zone until 1995 and it is still in the process of being demined. Kbal Spean is included in the Angkor ticket and is only open until 3pm; there is an additional road fee of 70,000 KHR for Phnom Kulen. *45km (28mi) northeast of Siem Reap, 12km (7mi) from Banteay Srei*

On the holiest mountains in the country: Buddha statue in Wat Preah Ang Thom

You can combine your excursion to Kbal Spean with a visit the German ACCB wildlife conservationists and their INSIDER TIP zoological breeding station for rare animals. *Angkor Centre for Conservation of Biodiversity | Kbal Spean | tel. 099 60 40 17 | www.accb-cambodia.org | 1.5 hour tour Mon–Sat 1pm, a small donation is appropriate*

PREAH VIHEAR ★ (129 E2) (*Ø G2*)

In a manner of speaking, the Preah Vihear, with its spectacular location on a precipitous spur of the Damrek Mountains, seems to dominate the far north of Cambodia. The temple (9th–12th century) is on Cambodian territory near the border with Thailand. In 2008, UNESCO declared Preah Vihear a World Heritage Site, but since then the border dispute that had been simmering for years has flared up once again and there is no end in sight. The sanctuary rises up via a series of naga staircases and four terraces like a throne of the gods, with *gopura* pavilions, columns, towers and galleries, to a height of almost 600m (2,000ft). From the ☀ top plateau the ground falls steeply away over a cliff, providing a breathtaking panoramic view across the empty and deserted countryside spread out at the feet of the visitors to the temple. The widespread mining of the area has resulted in there being hardly any settlements here.

For years, it was easier to reach this temple from Thailand, which led to masses of tour groups arriving from that country, and it is still hardly visited from Cambodia. However, the Thai border crossing has now been closed making this potentially one of the INSIDER TIP most peaceful and out-of-the-way UNESCO temple oases in all of Asia! A UN judgement was meant to secure peace in the area, but at the time of going to press, the Foreign Office was still warning against travelling to Preah Vihear – inform yourself of the current situation before departure. *5am–5pm | approx. 10,000 KHR | about 200km (125mi) northeast of Siem Reap, 6 hours on the new N 67 via Anlong Veng where many hotels are under construction*

ROLUOS GROUP (129 D3) *(ŵ G2)*

These three temples – *Bakong, Preah Ko* and *Lolei* – are remains of the city of Hariharalaya, the first large capital of the Khmer empire; named after Hari Hara, a Hindu god, it was founded by Jayavarman II in the 9th century. Within the space of 70 years, forerunners of the famous Angkor buildings were erected here, with sandstone, rather than wood and bricks, being used for the first time. The most impressive is the five-tier Bakong temple, built in 881 in honour of Shiva, with its ⚜ central hall in Angkor style (the *Independence Monument* in Phnom Penh is modelled on it) surrounded by eight towers, or what is left of them. To the north, the six Prasat towers of *Preah Ko* rise up, watched over by Nandi (Shiva's riding bull) guardian statues and stone lions. Conspicuously placed above many of the portals is Kala, a mythical creature with a large mouth and goggle eyes. *13km (8mi) miles east of Siem Reap on the N 6 towards Phnom Penh near the village of Roluos (some sections are currently being restored)*

WESTERN BARAY (129 C3) *(ŵ F2)*

While most of the irrigation reservoirs and moats from the Angkor epoch are now silted up or dried out, the 17 sq km (6.5 sq mi) western basin is still used. The power of the Khmer empire can be explained by their ability to control water and intelligent use of the monsoon periods. The Khmer kings had gigantic reservoirs laid out to make it possible to irrigate the fields worked by around 80,000 farmers in the dry season. In the rainy seasons, these basins filled with up to 40 million cubic metres (1,412 million cubic ft) of monsoon water that subsequently flowed down the natural incline to the fields via a sophisticated network of channels. This made it possible for the Khmer to have several rice harvests a year. Enjoy a boat cruise to the *West Mebon Temple* in the middle of the lake or have a picnic (you should probably not go swimming yourself in the less than tempting water and just watch the Khmer having fun). *N 6 beyond the airport, approx. 10km (6mi) west of Siem Reap and Angkor*

BATTAMBANG

(128 B4) *(ŵ F3)* **The second-largest town in Cambodia (pop. 160,000) is situated by the Sangker River. It's a picturesque place, with avenues, palms and frangipani trees between some magnificent pagodas.**

You will find many French-Chinese colonial buildings, such as the impressive governor's residence and typical shophouses, along the *riverfront* and bustling Street 3. The provincial capital is worth visiting to experience its tranquil, relaxed atmosphere after all the tourist bustle of Siem Reap only two and a half hours away by car, or as a stopover on the journey to or from Thailand. The morning is the best time to take a stroll through the market, the *Phsar Nath*, a pyramid-like ochre-yellow structure complete with clock tower in the modern Khmer architectural style that you can't fail to notice. The stacks of fruit, vegetables, rice and even jewellery will make you realise that this province, as Cambodia's granary, is one of the wealthiest and most fertile in the country.

FOOD & DRINK

In the afternoon, the soup kitchens of the Riverside Night Market fill up and serve their guests, sitting on plastic stools, simple Khmer fare (for hardly more than 5,000 KHR) including – for those who like them – grilled crickets.

WHITE ROSE

Always full, with a large selection of Khmer and Asian dishes (large servings for 10,000 KHR), friendly service. *Daily | Street 2, parallel to the western riverside road, near the Angkor Hotel | mobile tel. 012 53 65 00 | www.white rosebattambang.com | Budget*

SPORTS & ACTIVITIES

CYCLE, KAYAK AND BOAT TOURS

Cycle or paddle peacefully along – or on – the river, past old iron bridges and palms through an idyllic rural landscape where time seems to have stood still: along terraced vegetable fields, past bamboo stilt houses in fishing villages and temples, and through luxuriantly green scenery *(contact: Green Orange Kayaks | www.fedacambodia.org)*.

On one of the most beautiful boat trips in Cambodia, passengers chug along the Sangker River and across the enormous Tonle Sap Lake towards Siem Reap, past marshland, bird sanctuaries such as Prek Toal and countless houseboat settlements. The period from August to January is the best time for this excursion *(4–10 hours depending on the water level, not really recommended at the height of the dry season from March to May when there are often problems caused by overloading and running aground)*.

Family business Cambodian-style: stands in Battambang

PHARE PONLEU SELPAK (CIRCUS SCHOOL) 😊

Currently, around 100 children and teenagers, including about 30 orphans and street children, are being trained to be circus performers in this very committed training project and orphanage. In addition, they learn music, theatre and dance, painting and tailoring. The children enter into a kind of verbal contract after which they are permitted to work in the circus tent as clowns, magicians or trapeze artists. Visitors can watch the training, listen to the music and admire the exhibitions on weekdays between 8 and 11am, as well as between 2 and 5pm. *Shows: Thu 7–8pm followed by dinner (irregularly June–Oct) | approx. 30,000 KHR | Anh Chanh Village | around 1km west of the Vishnu Statue on the N 5, turn right onto a dirt road (signposted) | tel. 053 95 24 24 und 012 82 14 98 | www.phareps.org*

BAMBOO TRAIN

Travel like the Khmer: a fascinating one-hour trip on the most unique means of transport on rails, the *nori*. Just hop onto the bamboo-and-wood frame on wheels and the motor-powered buggy, which can reach speeds of up to 40kmph (25 mph) sets off along the bumpy track, laden not just with people but bags of rice, mopeds and even livestock. If another nori or freight train coming from Phnom Penh is encountered on the single-track railway, everybody just gets off and helps lift the frame from the tracks. Don't worry: the local train is even slower than the nori and only runs every couple of weeks (as long as the bridges on the route are intact; if not the nori service is also suspended). *From Ou Dambong, approx. 3km (2mi) south of the city centre and the east bank of the river (follow the signs) | all the fun costs approx. 20,000–35,000*

A trip on the Bamboo Train, Cambodia's answer to the rail trolley

KHR/person depending on the number of passengers or whether exclusively chartered for tourists | contact: the hotels or Local Adventures in Siem Reap | tel. 063 96 61 40 | www.local-adventures.com

MADISON CORNER

French cuisine, but specialising in countless varieties of crepes and salads, fast food, ice cream and all kinds of spirits, beer, cocktails and homemade rum. Also serves breakfast and milk shakes. *From 6am | Street 2.5, in the southwest of the market | Budget*

RIVERSIDE BALCONY

A beautiful old wooden house right on the river in almost jungle-like surroundings where they serve lots of simple western staples such as burritos and burgers, pasta and pizza, chilli con carne and 'Pork Schnitzel Robert'. The Riverside is a peaceful oasis in the afternoon but its bar becomes very crowded in the evening. Don't forget the mosquito repellent! *Tue–Sun 4–11pm | in the south of Battambang on the western bank (Street 1), corner of the N 57 towards Pailin | tel. 053 73 03 13 | Moderate*

Battambang is the city where the hotels offer the INSIDER TIP▶ best value for money.

LA VILLA

Some of the rooms in this colonial villa from the 1930s are enormous with ceilings supported by columns, as well as terraces and balconies; others are under the roof. They have a stylish mix of antique furniture (desks, chests four-poster beds, screens) and super-modern equipment (flat-screen TV, DVD). You enter room 2 through double Art Deco doors! Pool oasis in the garden, excellent restaurant with bar under an unusual glass-and-iron construction. *7 rooms | 185 Pom Romchek 5, eastern riverside road | tel. 053 73 01 51 | www.lavilla-battambang. net | Moderate*

ROYAL

Old and young meet in this well-tried three-storey hotel that provides excellent travel information. Individually decorated rooms (some with satellite TV, air-conditioning, warm-water shower). Magnificent panoramic view from the 🌿 roof terrace. *45 rooms | small street to the west of the market | tel. 053 95 25 22 and 016 91 20 34 | Budget*

STUNG SANGKE

Centrally located three-to-four-star hotel near the river; impressive lobby, elegant rooms, pool and fitness centre – but hardly any guests and, therefore, unbelievable price reductions. *130 rooms | N5 near the new north bridge | tel. 053 95 34 95 | www.stungsangkehotel.com | Moderate*

PHNOM SAMPEAU 🌿
(128 B4) (*Ш E3*)

According to the legend, the 160 m (525 ft) high mountain is the petrified broken hull of the ship on which the King of Siam once sailed with Princess Neang Rumsay Sok, whom he had abducted from the city of Takeo in the south of Cambodia. Once you have climbed up the 700 steps (20 minutes; but faster in a tuktuk) in the company of a few curious macaques and children you will be able to let your gaze wander over the green tops of the palm trees, the rice fields, the *Phnom Krapeu* (Crocodile Mountain) and the 400 m (1,300 ft) high plateau of *Phnom Banan* crowned by a five-towered temple dating from the 11th century (*25km/16mi south of Battambang*). Hidden inside Phnom Sampeau are several caves with Buddhist shrines, reclining Buddhas reaching nirvana, and two pa-

Every evening at sunset, the sky blackens during a spectacular natural phenomenon when ● INSIDER TIP ▶ thousands of bats swarm out of the caves on their nocturnal search for food. *Around 7,500 KHR | 12km (7mi) southwest of Battambang on the N57 towards Pailin*

Richly decorated pagodas crown the peak of the legendary mountain Phnom Sampeau

godas with frescoes. An almost macabre memorial site is located on the mountainside in the *Teng Klun Cave: the Killing Caves, Laang Kirirum,* preserved in honour of thousands of victims of the Pol Pot regime, including the monks, who were thrown to their death off the vertical cliffs here in the years between 1975 and 1979. A reclining Buddha watches over the bones and skulls kept behind glass in the cave; the scattered remnants of weapons (such as a Vietnamese flak gun) are silent witnesses to the time when the mountain was one of the Khmer Rouge's strategic strongholds.

INSIDER TIP ▶ **PRASAT WINE GROWING ESTATE PHNOM BANAN** (128 B4) (*ᗰ F3*)

Several thousand vines flourish on a hill near Phnom Banan – travellers find it hard to believe their eyes when they discover wine growing in Cambodia. For several years now, a Cambodian couple have devoted themselves to tending the delicate plants on the only estate in Cambodia which, until recently, operated using rather unusual methods such as burying the wine in plastic bottles in the sand to keep it cool while fermenting. You can taste the wine in the garden and also visit the cellars; connoisseurs should probably stick to grape juice. The tropical tipples (Shiraz, Cabernet Sauvignon and Chardonnay, as well as brandy) are sold here and in Battambang – look out for the pink label with the gold border. *10km (6mi) south of Battambang, along Route 155 on the west bank of the Stung Sangke towards Phnom Banan – somewhat difficult to find near the modern Wat Bai Dom Ram in the village of Bot Sala | tel. 012 66 52 38*

SIEM REAP

MAP ON PAGE 135
(128 C3) (*⌘ F2*) **No visitor to Cambodia will be able to avoid the boomtown Siem Reap – the city is, and always was, the starting point for all temple explorers.**

A frenzy of construction, a genuine gold rush fever, took hold of the small city (pop. 150,000) in the years around the turn of the millennium. And there is no end in sight: a never-ending line of hulking Angkor-Baroque-Fantasy hotels stretches all the way along Airport Road. Faced with the massive development of enormous complexes and golf courses

---

CITY **WHERE TO START?**
OLD MARKET (PHSAR CHAS)
(135 B3) (*⌘ b3*): Dive into the colourful hustle and bustle around the Old Market (Phsar Chas), between Khmer market women, fruit stands and ever-popular Pub Street with its jungle of advertising signs. Especially in the evening, this is the place to see and be seen and play billiards. There is no official public transport but any number of taxis, tuktuks, cyclos and co.

---

that has taken place (there were three hotels in Siem Reap in 1994; today, there are more than 200!) many critics see a repetition of the same problems that forced the Khmer Kingdom to dissolve 1,000 years ago: inadequate water supply, deforestation leading to too much water and flooding in the rainy seasons. It is now difficult to find the charming, traditional sides of Siem Reap behind the plethora of signs advertising pancakes, sushi, Angkor beer and karaoke. A few French colonial houses shaded by tamarind trees have managed to survive on the banks of the Stung Siem Reap. And, the time-honoured Grand Hotel d'Angkor, where Charlie Chaplin once laid his head, has risen like a phoenix from the ashes. Plundered by the Khmer Rouge in the 1970s, the legendary hotel is now rarely fully booked. If you take an excursion in the surrounding countryside – perhaps following the flow of the river for a few miles on a bicycle – you will pass through a rural world that has hardly changed in the past 100 years.

SIGHTSEEING

ANGKOR NATIONAL MUSEUM
(128 C3) (*⌘ F2*)

This is where you will get a very informative (but, unfortunately, also rather expensive) introduction before you visit the temple ruins. Many of the statues in Angkor itself are either copies or no longer exist, and this modern museum, complete with cinema *(shows every 15 minutes)*, presents a chronological exhibition of numerous statues of Buddha, busts of the Khmer kings, steles with historical inscriptions and other architectural fragments from different epochs. *Daily 8.30am– 6.30pm, except on holidays (shopping centre: daily 10am–8pm) | admission 45,000 KHR, plus Audio Tour Guide in Eng-*

lish 10,000 KHR | Vithei Charles de Gaulle, road to Angkor | www.angkornational museum.com

CAMBODIAN CULTURAL VILLAGE ●
(128 C3) (*∅ F2*)

Miniature copies of the most famous buildings in Cambodia, such as the Royal Palace in Phnom Penh, are on display in this model Khmer village. Visitors wander through the villages of the various ethnic groups in the country, such as the Chinese and Cham. Wax figures of famous personalities are also present – they include the Khmer kings, the parents of long-reigning King Sihanouk and national film stars. *Wedding Ceremony Show (daily 10.35am and 3.15pm)* at the *Millionaire's House*, a copy of a traditional teak villa. *Daily 9am–9pm | admission 40,000 KHR, free for children less than 3'7" | approx. 1km west of the town centre on the N6 towards the airport | restaurant with buffet dinner and show Fri–Sun 6.30pm | www.cambodian culturalvillage.com*

INSIDER TIP ▶ CONSERVATION D'ANGKOR
(128 C3) (*∅ F2*)

Thousands of valuable sculptures have been stored here, carefully guarded behind thick bars, for more than 100 years – it is said that there was a case of armed art theft at some time in the past. Entire archways and balustrades lean against the warehouse walls, phallic *linga* pedestals lie strewn all over the place, demons squat in a tidy row next to headless Buddhas and Shivas. The experts of *L´École française d´Éxtrême-Orient* collected these treasures during their restoration work in Angkor starting in 1908 until the French archaeologists were also forced to leave the land of the murderous Khmer Rouge in 1975. The warehouses with their estimated 6,000 objects are not really open to the public – but, you can try

to organise an appointment in advance (and sometimes one of the guards will open the door if you are friendly to him and make a small 'contribution'... The office of the *German Apsara Conservation Project (GACP, www.gacp-angkor.de)* is at the same location and workers or students are usually willing to give some information on the present status of the never-ending restoration work on Angkor Wat's 1,850 divine apsaras or devatas. *Daily 8am–6pm | Phum Traeng, a little bit out of town on the northern section of Pokambor St. by the Siem Reap River, Khum Slor Kram district | tel. 063 96 34 25 or mobile phone 012 94 30 96 (Director Tuon Phok)*

WAT BO (135 C3) (*∅ c3*)

One of the oldest and most venerated pagodas in Siem Reap containing magnificent old frescoes (late 19th century) with scenes from the Ramayana/Reamker saga, some of them magnificently coloured and not in the gaudy, kitschy style you see almost everywhere else. In the pictures look for, and then admire, the opium-smoking Chinese merchants and French soldiers watching the traditional apsara dances. Some old drums are also on display. *Mon–Thu 6am–6pm, Fri–Sun 4–5pm | Wat Bo St., near Theachamrat St.*

FOOD & DRINK

You can eat inexpensively and well all day long in the simple soup kitchens on the northern side of the Old Market *(Phsar Chas)* (135 B3) (*∅ b3*); the classic dishes of noodle soup, fried rice and fried noodles only cost around 7,500 KHR. Apart from that, a good 200 restaurants await custom in Siem Reap.

There are many pleasant new garden restaurants on Wat Bo Street on the east side of the river.

L'ANGELO (128 C3) (*ØØ F2*)
The exclusive Italian restaurant serves exquisite Northern Italian cuisine with a touch of Asia in a stylish ambience. *Daily | Vithei Charles de Gaulle, on the road*

and salmon. You can eat outside in the garden or indoors under ceiling fans and surrounded by greenery. *Daily | 729 Wat Bo St. | tel. 012 56 99 75 | www.selantra restaurant.com | Budget–Moderate*

There are still many colonial-style houses in the old section of Siem Reap

to Angkor Wat, 2km to the north | tel. 063 96 39 00 | Expensive

SAWADEE FOOD GARDEN
(135 C1) (*ØØ c1*)
Long-established, good Thai garden restaurant (roofed over and air-conditioned) run by a Thai family. You can choose your fish straight from a pool; the prices are not worth talking about. *Daily | Wat Bo St., approx. 50m north of the N 6 | tel. 063 96 44 56 | Budget*

SELANTRA (135 C3) (*ØØ c3*)
Modern Cambodian restaurant with unobtrusive, but chic, decor: a little bit away from the tourist area; friendly service and excellent Khmer cuisine with a French note. Interesting variety of salads, pizza and pasta, burgers and kebabs, steaks

THE SINGING TREE ☺
(135 B3) (*ØØ b3*)
Meeting place for the in-crowd, as well as families, this is an environmentally friendly garden idyll with rattan chairs, vegetarian dishes and seafood, cakes and ice cream. For the kids there are swings, sandpit, films, special food for children, hip-hop course; for the adults, a gallery, regular *monk chats* and yoga courses. *Closed Mon | Alley West, between Pub Street and the Old Market | tel. 092 63 55 00 | www.singingtreecafe. com | Budget–Moderate*

THE SUGAR PALM (135 A2) (*ØØ a2*)
Mainly delicious Khmer dishes are served in this traditional-style veranda house; you should also take a close list at the long wine list. Popular bar with very

cheap cocktails in the evening – and, no fixed closing time! *Sun closed | Taphul Road tel. 063 96 48 38 | Budget–Moderate*

VIROTH'S (135 C3) *(Ø c3)*

Amazingly inexpensive Khmer dishes and wines in a simple, but elegant, ambience: You dine between palm gardens and lapping ponds in this roofed open-air restaurant. *Daily | 246 Wat Bo St., behind the Residence Hotel | tel. 012 82 63 46 | www.viroth-hotel.com/restaurant.php | Budget–Moderate*

SHOPPING

Siem Reap could turn you into a shopping addict: in addition to the traditional (night-time) markets (don't forget to bargain!), there are hundreds of shops and – mainly along *Sivatha St.* – an increasing number of gigantic air-conditioned shopping centres (fixed prices).

OLD MARKET (PHSAR CHAS) ● (135 B3) *(Ø b3)*

Souvenir and bargain hunters can rummage around for hours between hundreds of stands with silk and silverware, arts-and-crafts, rattan furniture, statues of all sizes, traditional music instruments, *krama* cloths, jewellery, DVDs and CDs, as well as suitcases, handbags, household goods, mountains of fruit, fish and meat – all under a single roof in the centre of town. Remember, you have to bargain! You can buy trendy accessories and support a good cause at ☺ INSIDER TIP stand number 14 H 'Tooit Tooit': it belongs to the child-welfare organisation *Child Safe Network (Friends International)* and the profits are used to educate impoverished parents and street children. INSIDER TIP Stand number 14, run by the delightful Pisey, can also be recommended; she always offers fair prices for her

silk goods and jewellery, especially silver earrings.

Many boutiques, arts-and-crafts shops and galleries have opened up around the market. *6am to approx. 8pm, best prices in the morning | Pokambor Ave., on the west bank of the river*

ANGKOR COOKIES – MADAM SACHIKO (128 C3) *(Ø F2)*

Biscuits in the shape of Angkor with various aromas ranging from coffee to coconut to pepper, in addition to chocolate, fruit shakes, tea, coffee, palm sugar – all Cambodian products! There is also a small café on the premises. *Daily 9.30am–7pm | on the road to Angkor opposite the Sofitel Hotel | www.angkor cookies.com*

ANGKOR NIGHT MARKET (135 A3) *(Ø a3)*

The almost 200 arts-and-crafts stands selling souvenirs and unusual products made of water hyacinths, coconuts, rice paper and leather (shadow-theatre puppets) in their bamboo huts at the first Angkor Night Market guarantee *happy shopping*. There is also a 3D cinema and live bands perform occasionally in the straw-roofed Island Bar. *4pm–midnight | west of Sivatha St. | www.angkornight market.com*

ARTISANS D'ANGKOR ☺ (128 C3) *(Ø F2)*

The quality is astounding, and so are the prices: this education project began in 1992 and, since then, thousands of young Cambodians have received training in painting, stonemasonry, making pottery, weaving, etc. and now share in the profits. There are two branches: *Siem Reap: daily 7.30–6.30pm | Stung Thmey St. (with tours of the workshops)* and 16km (10mi) away in the *Angkor Silk*

Farm: daily 8am–5.30pm | with ● *free tours of the individual stages of production from the mulberry tree plantation to silk-worm breeding and silk weaving | there is also a museum on the premises | on the N6 towards Battambang | shuttle buses from the main branch at 9.30am and 1.30pm | tel. 063 96 33 30 | www. artisansdangkor.com*

BOOM BOOM ROOM (135 B3) (*ΩΩ b3*)

This place has everything to do with music: CDs, MP3 players and iPods, which you can also recharge here. With café serving good coffee and cakes. *Daily 10am–10pm | at the Old Market*

PICH REAMKER (135 B2) (*ΩΩ b2*)

You can purchase the completely hand-painted masks and spectacular golden headdresses used in traditional Ramayana/Reamker dances here. *Daily 7.30am–8.30pm | 591 Hup Guan St., behind the Central Market/Phsar Kandal*

SENTEURS D'ANGKOR (135 B3) (*ΩΩ b3*)

A fragrant symphony for the senses awaits you in this shop: spices, Khmer curry powder and coconut oil, handmade soap, bath salts and tiger balsam, tea, coffee and rice wine flavoured with cinnamon or ginger, joss sticks, legendary Kampot pepper and cashew nuts – all make attractive and tasty souvenirs. *Daily 7.30am–10pm | opposite the Phsar Chas | www.senteursdangkor.com*

SMATERIA ☺ (135 B3) (*ΩΩ b3*)

How about a chic handbag made out of a Tetra-Pak milk carton? Or a key fob of recycled plastic? The two Italians Elisa and Jennifer (helped by 50 Cambodian workers, some of them handicapped) demonstrate just what can be made out of fishing nets, waste plastic and other 'street material': creative and environmentally friendly! In *The Alley West, near Pub Street; there is also a shop at the Phnom Penh Airport | www.smateria.com*

The place to go for souvenir hunters: the Night Market in Siem Reap

SIEM REAP

INFORMATION

You can get information in all the guest-houses and hotels – and it is often better than in the official tourist office (opposite Raffles Hotel). The quarterly *Siem Reap Visitors Guide*, *Pocket Guide Siem Reap* and *Ancient Angkor Guidebook* can be obtained everywhere and are well worth reading.

SPORTS & ACTIVITIES

DR. FISH MASSAGES ●
(135 A3) (*ω a3*)

This ticklish Asian trend is a lot of fun, especially if your feet are worn out after visiting the temples. Dr Fish will take care of them: this trendy wellness institution and pedicure – with academic qualifica-tions – has tiny Garra Ruffa fish (also known as Kangal fish) nibble the calluses and scales off your feet (by the way, this kind of spa treatment originated in Tur-key and has been popular there since the 19th century). *Daily from 4pm | at the Angkor Night Market and other locations | tel. 017 41 24 75 | 20 min. from approx. 7,500 KHR*

FRANGIPANI SPA ● (135 B2) (*ω b2*)

One of the best spas in Siem Reap: gen-tle hands that exert just the right amount of pressure, soothing music, pleasant aromas, and a tamarind drink – this is the place to have yourself pampered styl-ishly with classical tropical massages *(60 min. 90,000 KHR)*, foot massages, herb-al baths, *Khmer Coffee Scrub* or facials *(Spa Package, 140 min., approx. 315,000 KHR | daily noon–10pm | 617 Hup Guan St., small street between the Riviera Hotel and Central Market/Phsar Kandal | tel. 063 96 43 91 | www.frangi panisiemreap.com)*.

COOKERY COURSE

If you want to get a closer look at what goes into Khmer woks and pots, you should book one of the trendy cookery courses with early-morning shopping at the market – e.g. from *Le Tigre de Papier* whose profits benefit a hotel school *(tel. 063 76 09 30 | www.letigredepapier.com | 3 hours 45,000 KHR)*, or with the popular *Cooks in Tuktuks* from the RiverGarden Restaurant *(3 hours 120,000 KHR | tel. 063 96 34 00 | www.therivergarden.info)*.

TOURS

ASIAN TRAILS (135 B2) (*ω b2*)

Professional tours from guides with many years of experience. *587 Hup Guan St. | tel. 063 96 45 95 and 063 96 45 96 | www.asiantrails.info*

BUFFALO TOURS (135 A2) (*ω a2*)

Experienced organisation offering all kinds of tours from the adventurous to luxurious including an 'elephant driving license' and bicycle rides from Saigon to Angkor. *556 Tep Vong St. | tel. 063 96 56 70 | www.buffalotours.com*

MONSOON TOURS (128 C3) (*ω F2*)

Specialised in birdwatching near Angkor, tours on the Mekong and to neighbour-ing countries. One of the oldest travel agencies in Cambodia. *030 Phnom Steng Thmey, Svay Donkom district | tel. 063 96 66 56 | www.monsoon-tours.com*

ENTERTAINMENT

With more than 100 bars, it's difficult to know where to start. The traveller com-munity congregates on *Pub Street* (just 50m north of the Old Market), which becomes a bustling pedestrian precinct in the evening. It is the location of such es-tablished institutions as *Angkor What?*

where you can dance until the early hours of the morning (sometimes on the tables) or play billiards *(from 6pm)*. If pensively, in the luxury hotels such as *Raffles (Mon, Wed and Fri | approx. 95,000 KHR)*.

Apsara dancers depict stories from the Cambodian world of legends

you're not interested in *beer girls* and gigantic screens showing the latest sporting events, drop in to one of the following:

APSARA THEATRE ⭐ (135 C3) (*ΩΩ c3*)

How about some culture? You can enjoy the famous apsara dances while having a dinner of traditional Khmer specialities in the large wooden pavilion of the Apsara Theatre. *Show daily at 8 and 9.30pm (1 May–15 Oct only Tue, Thu and Sat 7.30 pm) | approx. 80,000 KHR, reservations advisable | Wat Bo St., opposite the Angkor Village Hotel | tel. 063 96 35 61 | www.angkorvillage.com/theatre.php.* Other inexpensive performances are given in the *Butterfly Garden Restaurant* (*www.butterfliesofangkor.com*), the *Dead Fish Tower* and the *Temple Club (Temple Balcony, see low-budget tip)* or, more ex-

CAFÉ CENTRAL (135 B3) (*ΩΩ b3*)

There's something for all tastes in this restored colonial house (salads, soups, cakes) – and that is also the motto of the house's resident Filipino band. *Daily from 7am, live concerts from 9pm | northwestern corner opposite the Phsar Chas*

INSIDER TIP ▶ MISS WONG

(135 B3) (*ΩΩ b3*)

Here, you will feel yourself transported back to a tiny, relaxed opium den in old Shanghai as you sip your cocktails (the prices are a little high) between balloon lamps, calligraphy and bronze dragons. The host still shakes hands with all his guests when they arrive; you can fortify yourself with snacks such as *dim sum*. *Daily 5pm–1am | The Lane, parallel street north of Pub St.*

SORIA MORIA ROOFTOP BAR �▓
(135 C3) (*ʘ c3*)

The balmy breeze will refresh you as you watch the sun set from this rooftop or sip your cocktail in the heavenly bubbling Sky-Jacuzzi. Happy hour 5–8pm (on Wednesday, all drinks and tapas cost less than 5,000 KHR!). Trendy Khmer fusion cooking, Movie Night on Mondays, free dance show with the children from the ☺ *Sangkheum Center for Children* on Fridays. By the way, they also have wonderful rooms (*Moderate*). *Wat Bo St. corner of Street 24 | http://thesoriamoria.com*

THE RED PIANO (135 B3) (*ʘ b3*)

See and be seen; this is where Angelina Jolie and her film crew dropped by. That was a few years ago in 2000 but the service has remained good, the prices for international food and drinks are low and the atmosphere is great. The best view of the nocturnal activities is from the �▓ Veranda on the first floor – it is even better with a Tomb Raider cocktail in your hand. *Daily from 7am | Pub St. | tel. 063 96 47 50 | www.redpianocambodia.com*

WHERE TO STAY

ANGKOR STAR (135 B1) (*ʘ b1*)

Well-equipped and centrally located: the Cambodian hotel has spacious, comfortable rooms (TV, WiFi, minibar, coffee-tea machine, safe and – a rarity in this price category – hairdryer and iron!) and even a garden with a saltwater pool and sunbeds. If only the breakfast were better... *60 rooms | 54 Sivatha St. | tel. 063 76 69 99 | www.angkorstarhotel.net | Moderate*

ANGKOR VILLAGE CULTURAL HOTEL
(135 C3) (*ʘ c3*)

One of the best places to stay in Siem Reap: Khmer-style cottages (*Expensive*), a little close to each other, with four-poster beds and meticulously decorated in a small garden oasis, as well as some charming 'budget rooms' (*Moderate*). Without TV, but with WiFi, pool, business centre and cookery courses. *38 rooms | Wat Bo St. | tel. 063 96 33 61 | www.angkorvillage.com | Moderate–Expensive*

JOURNEYS WITHIN –
BED & BREAKFAST (128 C3) (*ʘ F2*)

Charming, small complex, suitable for families, with two-storey bungalows in a

LOW BUDGET

▶ The cheerful German-Cambodian couple who run *Chea's Guesthouse* in Siem Reap (128 C3) (*ʘ F2*) only charge 30,000–65,000 KHR for ship-shape rooms (satellite TV) including a generous breakfast and free bicycles (*18 rooms | N 6, about 2km east of the tourist centre of town/Old Market | tel. 012 36 22 40 | www.cheas-guesthouse.com*).

▶ Happy hour in the *Temple Club* in Siem Reap (135 B3) (*ʘ b3*) lasts all day long and a free Apsara dance show attracts price-conscious masses to the dinner buffet for an incredible 20,000 KHR (*7.30–9.30 pm | Pub St. | tel. 015 99 99 09*). There is another inexpensive show in the *Dead Fish Tower* on Sivatha St.

▶ Unbelievable but true, a room with all the trimmings in the *Khemara Hotel* (128 B4) (*ʘ F3*) in Battambang – complete with swimming pool – costs 55,000 KHR (*80 rooms | Street 515, 2km out of town | tel. 053 73 78 78 | www.khemarahotel.com*).

A legendary colonial home-away-from-home: Raffles Grand Hotel d'Angkor

large garden with a pool; a bit off the beaten track but that means it's peaceful. Interesting tours are offered and it's even possible to do volunteer work in one of the neighbourhood projects. *4 rooms | on the N6 towards the airport; after 4km turn off to the right after the Damnak Angkor Village Hotel | tel. 063 96 47 48 | www. journeyswithin.com | Moderate–Expensive*

LOTUS LODGE (128 C3) (*Ⓜ F2*)

This very popular complex offers rows of rooms very close to each other among palm trees, each with satellite TV and a miniature terrace. It has a large pool near the restaurant, plus billiards. There is a shuttle bus service to the centre (about 2km) twice a day. How about a **INSIDER TIP** romantic dinner in the old ☆ water tower with the lights of Angkor Wat sparkling in the distance? *36 rooms | Boeng Dounhpa Village, Slar-Kram-Commune | tel. 063 96 61 40 | www.lotus-lodge.com | Budget*

PALM VILLAGE RESORT & SPA (128 C3) (*Ⓜ F2*)

This idyllic bungalow complex in the countryside has seen better days and is definitely not suitable for nitpickers: the bamboo huts (with satellite TV and re-

frigerator) are spread among the palms, frangipani and mango trees in the luxuriant garden, showers flooded with light, pool and garden restaurant, ☆ observation tower. *16 rooms | Phum Trapaing Ses Village, on the N6 towards the airport, right turn after the Goldiana Hotel | tel. 063 96 44 66 | www.palmvillage.com.kh | Moderate*

RAFFLES GRAND HOTEL D'ANGKOR ★ (135 C1) (*Ⓜ c1*)

The journey through time begins as soon as you step into the silently floating *birdcage* lift: this hotel has paid host to sultans, Charlie Chaplin, Jacqueline Kennedy and many other VIPs since 1932. Magnificent rooms and suites with balconies in the original colonial building and in the new side wings, which look just as 'colonial', gigantic 35 m pool in the tropical garden, the most elegant restaurant in Siem Reap. 'High Tea', accompanied by piano music, is served every afternoon in the café ● *The Conservatory*. There are also special honeymoon arrangements such as 'couple massages', candlelit dinner in the temple with an apsara dance performance and personal butler or in the wonderful Cabana Suite with 'aphrodisiacal dishes'! *120 rooms and suites, 2 villas | Vithei Charles de Gaulle | tel. 063 96 38 88 | www.siemreap.raffles.com | Expensive*

SALINA HOTEL (135 A2) *(⌖ a2)*

Old-established hotel with comfortable rooms, pool, beer garden and karaoke – popular with tourist groups. *168 rooms | 125 Taphul Village, between Taphul St. and Psah Noe St. | tel. 063 76 04 87 and 063 76 04 89 | www.salinahotel.net | Moderate*

SHADOW OF ANGKOR II (135 C3) *(⌖ c3)*

In the centre of the tourist area: three-storey guesthouse under Cambodian management with lovely balcony rooms (satellite TV) and covered miniature pool, restaurant and bar. *20 rooms | Wat Bo St., at the corner of Street 25 | tel. 063 76 03 63 | www.shadowofangkor.com | Budget*

INSIDER TIP▶ SIEM REAP RIVERSIDE (128 C3) *(⌖ F2)*

A real bargain: this small hotel on the riverside offers peaceful bright rooms with ceiling fans or *air conditioning*, some with bathtub and satellite TV; rooftop bar, small restaurant, pleasant pool and free WiFi. Tours, discounts for Internet bookings. *20 rooms | southern section of Sivatha St., around 300m from the Old Market, near the Crocodile Farm | tel. 063 76 02 77 und 012 51 70 00 | www.siemreapriverside.net | Budget*

VIROTH'S HOTEL (135 C3) *(⌖ c3)*

Almost all of the minimalist furniture in the white miniature hotel, built in a modern Khmer architectural style, is made of natural stone (even the beds), bright rooms with terrace or balcony, small salt-water swimming pool and pleasant ☼ rooftop terrace with spa and Jacuzzi.

7 rooms. | Street 23, between River St. and Wat Bo St. near Theachamrat St. | mobile phone 012 77 80 96 | www.viroth-hotel.com | Moderate

WHERE TO GO

PHNOM KROM ☼ (128 C3) *(⌖ F3)*

You will be rewarded for climbing up the naga staircase to the approx. 140 m (460 ft) high Phnom Krom near the village of Chong Khneas with an idyllic sunset during which the sun makes the surrounding world of water glitter like gold. Yasovarman I had a temple erected here in honour of the three Hindu gods Shiva, Vishnu and Brahma in the 10th century and the three sandstone towers have remained standing until today. *12km (7mi) southwest of Siem Reap*

PREK TOAL (128 C3) *(⌖ F3)*

Not only ornithologists will be interested in making a day trip by boat to Prek Toak with its 'floating' villages and more than 100 different species of birds. The ☺ bird sanctuary (310 sq k/120 sq mi) is a haven for threatened storks, silver herons, grey pelicans, saurus cranes, ibises and sea eagles (the best time to visit is very early

in the morning or in the late afternoon from Dec/Jan–May/June). *Info: Sam Veasna Center for Wildlife Conservation at Wat Bo (www.samveasna.org) and the ecological tour organiser Osmose (day tour approx. 290,000 KHR | www. osmosetonlesap.net)*

TONLE SAP LAKE ★

(128–129 C–D 3–4) (𝄞 F–G3)

After a 12 km (7 mi) cycle tour to the south along the Siem Reap River with its wooden bridges – some are covered – and water wheels, small villages and pagodas in the shade of palm trees, stilt restaurants above rice fields and wide lotus ponds, you will reach the Tonle Sap Lake. The aquatic world of this gigantic lake, a biosphere reserve, glitters in the sun during and after the rainy season. Every year, when the mighty river can no longer contain the masses of monsoon rain and melted water from the Himalayas, its tributary, the Tonle Sap, changes direction and flows backwards into the Tonle Sap Lake which increases its normal size fivefold (from around 2,500 to 12,000 sq km/950 to 4,600 sq mi). This miracle of nature supposedly makes the Tonle Sap the lake with the most abundant fish stocks on the planet, which are however threatened by over-exploitation. When the water recedes in the dry season, they follow it in their houseboats in 'floating villages'. There is a Cambodian saying: *Mean toek, mean trey* (where there is water, there are fish). Others live in stilt-house settlements such as those in *Chong Khneas* (pop. 8,000) and *Kampong Phluk* (pop. 3,000; both are overrun in the high season), where an ancient method is used to adapt the houses to the water level – something like a lift, with ropes simply anchoring the bamboo floor at a higher or lower level. The rather poor settlement of *Kampong Khleang* (ca. 50km/30mi southeast of Siem Reap), with its up to 10-m (32-ft) high stilt 'skyscrapers' is not as popular with tourists; it is easy to see the houses in the dry season but then the smell is less than sweet… Boat trips and kayak tours (the best time: Aug–Dec) make it possible for tourists to explore this ● amphibian universe of 'floating' villages and floodplain forests. *(Information: p. 78 'Tours' or www.journeyswithin.com | day tour approx. 160,000 KHR/person).* Or would you prefer a dinner cruise on the *Tara Boat (www.taraboat.com)*?

Stilt houses in a unique natural wonder – the vast Tonle Sap Lake

ALONG THE MEKONG

A world full of magical, almost surreal, impressions awaits visitors to the Mekong: in the rainy season, forests submerged in a labyrinth of channels and islands – and fish swimming in the treetops. In contrast, dust red tracks are typical of the Ratanakiri and Mondulkiri provinces in the east of the country that were so isolated for decades.

Tourists are always enchanted by the provincial atmosphere of the small riverside towns of Kratie and Stung Tereng. Their charm lies in the leisurely way you can go with the flow on boats and in the markets and come into contact with fishermen and monks. You can get a better idea of everyday life in the country by spending time in the monasteries or on homestays. And, the last Irrawaddy freshwater dolphins in Cambodia still frolic near Kratie.

On a trip to Ratanakiri and Mondulkiri tourists will encounter natural wonders as well as minority peoples who, in some of the remoter villages, still live light years away from modern, 21st-century Cambodia. Their ancient traditions and property are threatened – as is the habitat of the last wild elephants: in both provinces, the ethnic groups are losing their land to powerful speculators – for lucrative gemstone mines, rubber and cashew-nut plantations, for casinos and golf courses. The investors are ready and waiting in the wings. The main attraction in Ratanakiri is gibbon watching but the wonderful landscape around Mondulkiri with elephant trekking and the largest

Photo: Fishermen on the Mekong

A vast river and red earth – you will find unspoilt nature and old traditions off the beaten track

waterfall in the country also has significant potential for tourism.

BAN LUNG (RATANAKIRI)

(131 D2) (*K2*) **Eighty percent of the people living in Ratanakiri Province in the far northeastern corner of the country come from minority ethnic groups: the Khmer Loeu who live from their fru-** **gal harvests on the rice and vegetable fields; some of them still practice the animistic traditions of their forefathers.** Adventurous nature lovers set out from the dusty province capital city Ban Lung (pop. 30,000) to go trekking in the jungle of *Virachay National Park* or swimming in the fabulous *Yaklom crater lake* or under impressive waterfalls.

Visitors to the area should bear one thing in mind: in Ratanakiri, it is either so dry that they will always be coated with rust-red dust or so wet that they will sink into

Village life on stilts in a Kreung settlement in Ratanakiri

the mud on many roads (trekking can not really be recommended in the rainy season from April/May to October but motocross riders swear that the muddy tracks are only really 'challenging' then...). You can continue your trip from this Cambodian no-man's-land to Vietnam, which is only about 80 km (50 mi) away, but you should be sure to get a visa beforehand.

FOOD & DRINK

BOEUNG KAMSAN RESTAURANT
Open-air terrace restaurant on Kamsan Lake serving Khmer, Thai and other Asian specialities, in three serving sizes! *Daily | on the road to Voen Sai | Budget–Moderate*

GECKO HOUSE
Rustic bar-restaurant with rattan chairs and decking. Asian food, tofu burgers and spaghetti accompanied by Heineken beer and good music. *Daily | parallel road south of the N 78, main road | Budget*

SPORTS & ACTIVITIES

KAYAK TOURS
Kayaking against the current on *Tonle San River* as far as the *Cemetery of the Tampuan* including a fortifying picnic on the sandbank *(bookings, e.g. through Terres Rouges Lodge)*.

ENTERTAINMENT

RIK'S CAFÉ CAMBODGE
Relax in rattan furniture with good music and a wonderful ✵ panoramic view; share information while tucking into typical travellers' fare; breakfast until noon. *On the 'Pub Street', parallel street to the N 78, next to Dutch Co Trekking Agency | Budget*

WHERE TO STAY

LAKESIDE HOTEL ✵
Perfect panoramic view: six of the decent rooms (with satellite TV) in the three-sto-

rey hotel have balconies overlooking the lake. *24 rooms | on the southwest shore of Kanseng Lake | tel. 012 72 22 96 | Budget*

PHNOM YAKLOM MOTEL (MOUNTAIN TOP HOTEL)

Well-tended retreat on a hilltop consisting of a modern hotel block and traditional wooden bungalows with bright rooms and a lot of wood, TV. At sunset, guests having drinks or dinner can enjoy the INSIDER TIP idyllic panorama from the veranda. Occasional folklore shows around a campfire. Free bicycles, moped rental and pick-up service. *18 rooms | Phnom Yaklom, approx. 1km from Yaklom Lake, 5 km (3 mi) from Ban Lung | tel. 012 68 88 87 and 011 67 77 71 | phnomyaklom. com | Budget–Moderate*

NORDEN HOUSE

Living IKEA-style: Scandinavian-Cambodian guesthouse with clean bungalows, garden terraces (DVD, ceiling fans, electricity 6pm–6am). Motorbike and trekking tours, sauna! *6 rooms | on the road to Yaklom Lake, 4 km (2.5 mi) east of Ban Lung | mobile tel. 012 88 03 27 | www. nordenhouseyaklom.com | Budget*

TERRES ROUGES LODGE

Stylish, wooden former governor's villa, the rooms furnished with Cambodian 'antiques' (some with a view of the lake, flat-screen TV); also three luxurious bungalows with bathrooms open to the sky. Pool and spa in the garden, very good international restaurant *(Moderate)*. Book well in advance! *23 rooms | on the east shore of Kanseng Lake | tel. 012 77 06 50 | www.ratanakiri-lodge.com | Moderate*

YAKLOM HILL LODGE

Simple, slightly drab, eco-huts – damp in the rainy season but it doesn't get more idyllic and secluded than this. ☺ Solar electricity 6–9pm. Much information on tours, Thai garden restaurant, *(Budget)*, footpaths up a 🌿 hill with fine views. *15 rooms | 5 km (3 mi) east of Ban Lung, near Yaklom Lake | tel. 011 79 05 10 | www. yaklom.com | Budget*

WHERE TO GO

KHMER LOEU VILLAGES
(131 D–E2) (*Ø K–L2*)

A dozen different highland tribes live in Ratanakiri Province, including the *Tampuan, Kreung, Jarai* and *Brou*, about 60,000 people in all. This is where the modern age meets an ancient way of life

The members of the highland clans are wary of strangers

with traditions such as using fire to clear the land and hunting with poison arrows. However, the fashion-conscious Khmer Loeu woman now wears her sarong with a top or at least a bra, and only a few of older Brou women sport face tattoos and heavy earrings. The belief in water, fire and forest spirits, as well as water buffalo sacrifices and ancestral worship, is still widespread. It is believed that the spirits live in the east and, for this reason, people always sleep facing in that direction, and the rice-wine jugs – the most-prized possession in any household – are also stored in the eastern corner. The traditional bamboo huts are gradually giving way to the typically Khmer stilt huts and stone houses. The fragile-looking 'boys' huts mounted on posts up to 5 m (16 ft) high (only Nov–April) and the smaller 'girls' huts, where the two sexes get together during puberty, are a special feature of Kreung villages (there are also copies of these 'love' huts at Yaklom Lake). The Kreung are very shy with strangers: on no account should you photograph the children – they believe that their spirit will be captured on a photo!

The following **INSIDER TIP** villages can be recommended for day trips: for the Kreung culture, *Krala* and *Kres* (Poi community), as well as *La Ak* (Ochum district); the Tampuan villages of *La En Kraen* and *Katae* where longhouses on stilts have been preserved *(60km/37mi northeast, near Andong Meas);* and the Jarai houses in *Borkeo*. The Dutch-Cambodian DutchCo Trekking Tours agency, run by Rik and Ivonne, organises these trips as well as canoe tours *(3-day trek from 365,000 KHR/person | parallel road south of the N78/main road | tel. 097 6 79 27 14 | www.trekkingcambodia.com).*

TAMPUAN CEMETERY
The burial rituals of the Jarai and Tampuan are famous. A visit to one of the Tempuan cemeteries that is open to the public is nothing for the faint-hearted. Water buffaloes are sacrificed in the *Kap Krabei Pheok Sra* ceremony and you will find one or more buffalo heads and skins hanging on the overgrown tombs between colourful wooden statues (usually depicting the deceased's trade), elephant tusks carved out of wood and offerings

such as rice baskets, creels and gongs. The cemetery opposite the village of *Ka-chon* around 40 km (25 mi) northwest of Ban Lung is particularly worth visiting *(bookings for half-day tours with boat trip on the Tonle San River through the hotels | admission approx. 5,000 KHR).*

VIRACHAY NATIONAL PARK ★
(131 D–E 1–2) (*Ø K–L 1–2*)

At night you will hear the chirp of the crickets, in the early morning the call of the gibbons as you gently swing in your hammock beneath the starry sky. Trekking tours through the Virachay National Park *(around 50 km/31 mi north of Ban Lung)* are guaranteed to give you a really close encounter with nature and an adventurous time. Your route through the jungle will take you near the former Ho Chi Minh Trail, past remote Khmer Loeu villages, crossing rivers and streams on suspension bridges or navigating them by kayak and raft. Covering an area of 3,325 sq km (1,284 sq mi) this is the largest national park in the country, encompassing both dense jungle and grass savannah; the highest elevation is the 1,500 m (5,000 ft) *Phnom Yak Youk*. On a one-week trek through the isolated *Phnom Veal Thom Wilderness,* you will have a good chance of encountering sambar and muntjac deer, gibbons, rare douc langur monkeys, as well as hornbills. Tigers, elephants and kouprey ox usually stay in hiding. Best trekking season: Dec–May; it is essential to have protection against malaria (mosquito repellent, long-sleeved light-coloured clothing, emergency medication) and never touch any piece of metal you see on the way – it could be a remnant of an unexploded bomb! *(A four-day tour for two costs approx. 500,000 KHR/person | National Park office: Mon–Fri 8am–noon and 2–5pm | southeast of Kanseng Lake*

in Ban Lung, on the N78, turn north/left near the post office | Ranger Thon Soukhon (English) | mobile tel. 012 36 36 89 (Mr Chou Sophark) | Information about trekking tours, etc: viracheyecotourism. blogspot.com).

WATERFALLS & ELEPHANT RIDES ●
(131 D2) (*Ø K2*)

You will probably be impressed not so much by the height of the *Katieng Waterfall* (10 m/33 ft) as by the possibility of coming right up to its cascade on the back of an elephant *(from Kateung village | a 1-hour ride costs approx. 40,000 KHR | 7am–5pm | approx. 6km/4mi west of Ban Lung).* Most beautiful of all is the 20 m (66 ft) high *Kachang Waterfall (around 500 m beyond the Katieng Waterfall),* where the Khmer like to come at the weekend to shower and swim in the large natural pool. The lovely cascade of the

Gibbons can often be heard faraway in the jungle

Cha Ong Waterfall is about the same height; here you can have a picnic behind the veil of water, drink rice wine or climb up the steep stairway to the bathing pool. On your way back you can scale the small ❄️ temple mountain *Eisey Patamak* (also: *Phnom Svay*) with the *Wat Aran* and its reclining Buddha; there is a wonderful view of Ban Lung from the hill, especially at sunset *(approx. 1km west of Ban Lung on the N 78).*

YAKLOM LAKE ⭐ (131 D2) *(𝄞 K2)*

The Boeung Yaklom is a circular, blue crater lake lying in an idyllic dense forest. There are three bathing platforms; however, out of respect for the modestly-dressed Khmer swimming and picnicking here, women should bathe in a sarong or shorts and t-shirt. A path to the right leads to the Cultural and Environmental Center with an exhibition, everyday articles used by the Jarai and Tampuan, and a souvenir stand. *7am–5.30pm | entrance fee 2,500 KHR | approx. 5km (3mi) east of Ban Lung | children's swim vests are also available | snack booths*

KRATIE

(130 C5) (𝄞 J4) **The small town of Kratie (pronounced: Kratshay; pop. 80,000) gives a good impression of everyday life on the Mekong – with lots of bustling activity between the harbour, markets and colonial buildings.**

You can relax on benches under gigantic trees along the riverside promenade and enjoy the sunset – perhaps over a bowl of *num ban jork* noodle soup from one of the cookshops. Apart from quite a few statues of animals, Kratie doesn't have much in the way of interesting sights. Most visitors come to see the ● rare Mekong dolphins that live in this area.

SIGHTSEEING

WAT ROKA KANDAL

This pretty pagoda, with its wood-and-tile roof and frescoes, in the more than 100-year-old Wat Roka Kandal, is one of the last to have been preserved in Kratie. Inside, handicrafts – mainly baskets and pottery, as well as silk – are sold between the decorated pillars. *Daily 8am–5pm (the pagoda might be closed) | 2km south of the centre on the river | information: Guide Mr Sothea (tel. 011 55 40 56)*

FOOD & DRINK

LE BUNGALOW

The best restaurant in town: French cuisine, pizza, Khmer classics, excellent wine list and cocktails. Some stylish rooms can be rented in the villa *(Moderate). Road along the river | tel. 089 75 80 90 | Moderate*

RED SUN FALLING

Joe pampers his guests in his house on the riverbank with western and local food, cakes and pastries and a large selection of alcoholic drinks. *Road along the river, in the centre | tel. 011 28 58 00 | Budget*

STAR RESTAURANT

Popular meeting place for backpackers: the food, from salads over sandwiches to fried rice and curries, is good and plentiful. Excellent range of alcoholic drinks. *On the south side of the market | tel. 012 75 34 01 | Budget*

SPORTS & ACTIVITIES

CYCLE TOUR ON KOH TRONG

An interesting 10-km (6 mi) cycle tour on the ⟨INSIDER TIP⟩ Koh Trong island in the river: the circular route passes a 'floating' village with Vietnamese fishing families, stupas and monasteries such as the *Wat Tov Te Ang*, a Chinese cemetery and gardens. *Regular trips from the Night Market or boat charter from the pier in Kratie (ca. 7,500 KHR) | homestay information for Koh Trong: tel. in Kratie c/o KAFDOC 011 55 40 56 and 012 91 96 13 (guide), tel. in Phnom Penh 023 35 72 30 | www.ccben. org, www.mekongdiscoverytrail.com and www.crdt.org.kh*

WHERE TO STAY

SALA KOH TRONG
Accommodation on a small island in the middle of the river. The stilt house with restaurant (half-board) accommodates its guests in nicely decorated rooms with simple wooden furniture (shared bathroom on the first floor; en-suite downstairs). Electricity 6–11pm. In addition there are ten luxurious stilt bungalows next door, as well as a pool. *15 rooms | Koh Trong (island) | tel. 012 77 01 50 | www.kohtrong.com | Budget–Moderate*

SANTEPHEAP HOTEL
Large Khmer hotel with decent rooms, some with a view of the river, good res-

taurant *(Budget)*. *40 rooms | on the riverside | tel. 072 97 15 37 | Budget–Moderate*

WHERE TO GO

IRRAWADDY DOLPHINS
(130 C4) (*Ø J3*)
In the dry season, the last 85 Cambodian freshwater dolphins *(Orcaella brevirostis)* congregate in the remaining deep-water pools in the Mekong. The most popular way to observe them is on a 🚤 boat tour from Kampi – however, you'll probably manage to spot the head of a single animal. Ask your helmsman to turn off the motor as soon as you reach one of the pools – otherwise, you'll have no chance of seeing anything at all (on holidays in particular, the stilt restaurants directly on the Mekong at the Kampi Rapids just to the north are unbelievably crowded). If you don't want to be part of disturbing the dolphins with all the commotion caused by the boats, you can attempt glimpse the rare animals through your binoculars from the platform in Kampi – the best time is early in the morning or late in afternoon between December and May. The endan-

You will need luck to see the Irrawaddy freshwater dolphins near Kratie

gered dolphins are further threatened by fishing using dynamite, electroshocks and river-wide dragnets, as well as pesticides and dam construction. *Boat for 2 persons (1 hour): 35,000 KHR/person /14km (9mi) north of Kratie | www.me kong-dolphin.com*

INSIDER TIP Other places for dolphin watching: *Koh Phdau (50km/31mi north of Kratie)*, *Damrei Phong*, *Koh Krouch* and *Kroh Preah (12km/7mi and 20km/12mi south of Stung Treng, respectively)*, *Anlong Cheuteal (with boats)* and *Anlong Svay on the Laotian border.*

One of the largest temples in Cambodia: Wat Sambour

WAT SAMBOK ● (130 C4) (*ơ J3*)
160 steep steps, guarded by *krak* warriors, lead visitors up to the Wat Sambok monastery and its two small pagodas on the top of the hill of the same name. In addition to pictures from the life of Buddha, visitors will be able to look at horrifying scenes of hell – as colourful as they are sadistic – in an open pavilion on the crest of the hill. There is a wonderful 360-degree panoramic view of the surrounding rice fields, Kratie and the Mekong from the ⚘ pagoda higher up on the right (another 200 steps). *Around 10km (6mi) north of Kratie*

WAT SAMBOUR ★ ● (130 C4) (*ơ J3*)
One of the largest and most modern temples in the country: Wat Sambour (also: *Sorsor Moi Roi*) was reconstructed in 1997 after the Khmer Rouge had destroyed the more-than-400-year-old monastery. It is also known as the '100 Column Monastery'; today, 116 columns support the vihara. The golden *Royal Stupa* (supposedly built in 1529) where, according to a legend, the ashes of a princess are kept, has been preserved. *35 km (22 mi) north of Kratie*

INSIDER TIP It is possible to spend some time in *Wat Sambok* (women only) and *Wat Sambour* in return for a small donation; however, this can only be seriously recommended for those who are really interested or experienced Buddhists. *(Information Wat Sambok: Vipassana Dhura Meditation Center: phnomsambok.blog spot.com/2010/11/wat-phnom-samboks-views-kratie-province.html, information Wat Sambour: tel. 011 76 88 47 and 011 71 63 11 or in the hotels).* A homestay with a family is also possible on the Mekong island *Koh Phdau* around 10km (6mi) to the north *(10,000 KHR/person; very simple without much privacy | locally: tel. Mr Sok Sim 099 54 62 53 and 011 70 93 29 |*

www.ccben.org | in Phnom Penh tel. 023 35 72 30 | www.crdt.org.kh), with dolphin watching and bullock cart tour (information: tel. 099 83 43 54 | www.crdt.org.kh).

SEN MONO-ROM (MON-DULKIRI)

(131 E5) (⌑ K4) Mondulkiri has one of Cambodia's most fascinating landscapes, but it is also amongst the poorest and most remote regions in the country.

The jolting ride past gigantic dipterocarp trees, through dense forests that gradually soften into a gently rolling hilly landscape with conifers and grassland at an altitude of around 900 m (2,900 ft), will be the first fascinating impression you have of this enormous, little visited, province. There has only been electricity in Sen Monorom (pop. 20,000), the drowsy provincial capital without many sights of interest, since 2008. You can take a ride on the backs of what were once working elephants to the waterfalls and villages of the highland peoples, mainly the *Phnong*.

FOOD & DRINK

BANANAS
The hostess Tanya serves hearty home-style cooking in her garden restaurant. Beef in beer sauce, ribs of pork with sauerkraut, and chateaubriand. *A few hundred metres northeast of the main road | tel. 092 41 26 80 | Budget–Moderate*

KHMER KITCHEN
Sitting amongst the plants in the courtyard you can choose from a colourful, international range of options, from amok to burritos, spaghetti and pancakes; speciality: Cambodian BBQ. *On the main road opposite to the Sovann Kiri Guesthouse | Budget*

SHOPPING

MIDDLE OF SOMEWHERE
Bill sells textiles, wickerwork and coffee made by the *Phnong*, who are also trained to be guides here *(approx. 90,000 KHR/day)*, in his café. *On the main street opposite the Holiday Guesthouse | tel. 012 47 48 79 | www.bunongcenter.org*

WHERE TO STAY

MONDULKIRI HOTEL
Mondulkiri's first 'luxury hotel': the two wooden bungalows (satellite TV, refrigerator) are particularly suited to nature lovers, although they are extremely over-

LOW BUDGET

▶ The bright corner-rooms *(40,000–55,000 KHR)* and the five bungalows in the garden with a view of the lake *(75,000 KHR)* in *Lakeside Chheng Lok* in Ban Lung **(131 D2) (⌑ K2)** can be recommended; but the rooms, with ceiling fans, facing the (quiet) street are unbeatably economical – not even 20,000 KHR! *41 rooms | at Kanseng Lake | tel. 012 95 74 22*

▶ Thrifty travellers to *Stung Treng* **(130 J2) (⌑ J2)**, who have nothing against cold showers, can stay in the hospitable *Ly Ly Guesthouse* – some of the rooms even have a balcony and satellite TV – for 25,000–60,000 KHR. *25 rooms | on the east side of the market | tel. 012 93 78 59*

priced (discounts are possible). Good, inexpensive restaurant *(Budget)*. *50 rooms | on the main road, turn left at the hospital | tel. 012 77 70 57 | www. mondulkiri-hotel.com | Moderate*

NATURE LODGE ☀

A hospitable ecologically friendly retreat with a lot of cats, chickens and ponies: very simple huts built on piles with garden bathrooms (hot water) and beautiful views through the sliding glass doors and from the veranda. *15 rooms | approx. 2km northeast of the main road, turn right at the hospital | tel. 012 23 02 72 | www.naturelodgecambodia.com | Budget*

WHERE TO GO

BOU SRA WATERFALL ★
(131 E5) (*ΔΔ L3*)

Right in the middle of the jungle, the highest waterfall in the country cascades over two stages (20m and 30m) – into a pool at the bottom (you have to cross the bridge at the car park to reach the steep steps on the other side of the cascade). There are some food stands. *Entrance fee 5,000 KHR | 37 km (23 mi) east of Sen Monorom, some sections of the road are bad*

INSIDER TIP▶ ELEPHANT VALLEY PROJECT ☀ (131 E5) (*ΔΔ K4*)

Old and wounded working pachyderms have found a sanctuary in this elephant camp. The strenuous, bumpy drive to the Phnon village is more than compensated for by the sight of the elephants in the dense jungle in the valley. Check beforehand to find out if there are enough elephants for everybody to take a ride through the jungle. Accommodation is possible in four replicas of the unique, traditional Phnong houses with their low thatched roofs and terracotta floors, decorated with old chests and photographs of elephants,

hot-water showers – the loveliest place to stay in Mondulkiri! There is some less expensive backpacker accommodation next door *(tel. 012 22 82 19 (9am–5pm | www. elephantvalleyproject.org | both Budget).* One-day elephant ride or elephant 'driving' course with or without an overnight stay: 185,000 KHR/person (children 90,000 KHR) | Pon Trom Village (also: Poutrou) | approx. 10 km (6 mi) west of Sen Monorom*

PHNONG VILLAGE: PUTANG
(131 E5) (*ΔΔ K4*)

It is also possible to go for elephant rides with a mahout in Putang and other Phnong (also: *Bunong*) villages – they have bred elephants for generations. However, your expectations should not be too great: also here, there are only a few traditional houses with their thatched roofs that almost reach the ground and it is rumoured that the women quickly deck themselves out with their heavy earrings when tourists are on the way… If a Phnong-speaking guide arranges for you to have a conversation with one of the village elders, you will find out a lot of interesting facts about their old traditions such as teeth filing, animism, music and medicine. *Rides 8am–3pm | five-hour elephant ride approx. 75,000 KHR/person | approx. 11 km (7 mi) southwest of Sen Monorom, preferably with a guide*

INSIDER TIP▶ SREPOK WILDERNESS
(131 E4) (*ΔΔ K–L3*)

The Srepok Wilderness in the region to the north of Sen Monorom is one of the last, vast (almost) uninhabited areas of Southeast Asia. With its with cascades, caves and rare wildlife it attracts adventurers and ornithologists to take daylong tours on foot, in kayaks, on mountain bikes or elephants. Ecotourism is still in its infancy or 'pilot phase' but the WWF is already planning a trekking lodge.

It is already possible to explore the *Srepok River Discovery Trail* (1.5 km) near nature conservation area. Adventure seekers can take part in the everyday life of the village, watch the people weaving, swim in the river (you wash there too – but, keep your sarong on ladies!), quaff

Phnong village of Putang: this family still lives in one of the traditional houses

Sen Monorom, preferably armed with a WWF brochure telling you how to look for eagles or the conspicuous Indian Roller *(Coracias beghalensis)*, termites, porcupines and monkeys. Kingfishers, turtles and otters have their homes on the riverbanks and you might even catch a glimpse of a Siamese crocodile. As many animals, including the sambar or muntjak deer, are only active at night, you should look out for the specific trails and tracks and try to identify their typical cries from afar.

The WWF's ☺ *Dei Ey Community Homestay Project (46km/29mi north of Sen Monorom on the N76) is located between the Phnom Prich Wildlife Sanctuary* (2,250 sq km/870 sq mi) and the *Mondulkiri Forest* (4,000 sq km/1,545 sq mi)

rice wine with the Phnong in the evening and spend the nigh in simple accommodation or under the stars in your hammock at the WWF Camp on the O Chbar River. There is even a chance that you will come across gaur and banteng wild oxen, the biggest herd of wild elephants in Cambodia, or the yellow-cheeked gibbon *(Nomascus gabriellae)* that is threatened with extinction on one of the tours lasting up to three days. The few wary leopards are more likely to come out at night (in 2007, a leopard mother and her cubs were caught for the first time in a 'camera trap' in the Srepok Wilderness and, years ago, rangers also saw and photographed a tiger). *Information: WWF office on the main road in Sen Monorom | tel. 073 6 90 00 96 and 012 46 63 43 |*

www.mondulkiritourism.org or from Mr Sam Nang in the Greenhouse Restaurant & Bar | tel. 017 90 56 59 | www.greenhouse-tour.blogspot.com (also motorbike tours) or from Vanny the tour guide | tel. 011 35 18 41 | tuonvanny@gmail.com

STUNG TRENG

(130 C3) (*Ø J2*) ★ A small jewel where the Mekong and Sekong meet: the provincial capital Stung Treng (pop. 40,000) near the Laotian border is neglected by most of the tourists hurrying to reach the neighbouring country.

This is a mistake, because it is possible to experience the most idyllic aspects of Cambodia in this charming town – on a cycle tour along the river with the old wooden houses under palm trees and groves of bamboos, on homestays with the local farmers and on kayak tours or boat trips on the Mekong to fishing villages and through enchanted flooded forests. Who can tell how long this idyll will last – the bridge over the Sekong was opened in 2008 and it is envisaged that tranquil Stung Treng will develop into the hub between China, Laos, Vietnam and Thailand.

SIGHTSEEING

WAT KHAT TAKYARAM

The most beautiful of the three monasteries on the riverside road is the Wat Khat Takyaram (also: *Wat Kandal*) with magnificent burial stupas and a delicate, two-storey pagoda with wall paintings: peaceful scenes from the life of Buddha at the front and scenes of torture in hell at the back. *A little to the east of the Gold River Hotel*

FOOD & DRINK

The Night Market and the soup kitchens along the banks of the Sekong offer local food at sensational prices. If you need something to eat on the go, some villages in the vicinity specialise in *krolan*, a typical Asian snack made of sticky rice with coconut milk and soya beans in bamboo canes. Or try the grilled sweet bananas coated with sticky rice and wrapped in banana leaves and – if you are brave enough – the small *nhem* packages (spicy, raw fish in banana leaves).

RIVERSIDE

Everybody comes here: backpackers and culture vultures. The dynamic Mr Thea dishes up travel tips, local and western food, breakfast and bicycles in this restaurant. *Near the road along the river behind the petrol station and bus stop | tel. 011 60 03 81 and 012 49 03 33 | Budget*

SOUN THA

Large restaurant – very popular with the locals – with many tasty dishes. There is an English menu; however, none of the staff speaks it and you might have to rely on the helpful English-speaking Khmer at the next table. *Street 63 (N 7), a few steps south of the market | Budget*

ENTERTAINMENT

How about a ❋ **INSIDER TIP** side trip to Sunset Point at *Wat Thom Raing Sey* at the confluence of the Mekong and Sekong to experience the idyllic meditative atmosphere as the sun sinks fiery red into the Mekong while the monks start chanting their pali prayers? This is how places of enlightenment must be! *Approx. 3 km (2 mi) west of the centre*

ALONG THE MEKONG

WHERE TO STAY

GOLDEN RIVER HOTEL (TONLE MEAH) ﹏

The best place in town with three floors of comfortable rooms (bathtub, satellite TV, refrigerator) and views of the river. Unfortunately no restaurant; breakfast is served in the Riverside Guesthouse approx. 200 m to the west. *36 rooms | on the road along the river | tel. 012 98 06 78 | www.goldenriverhotel.com | Budget*

WHERE TO GO

MEKONG BLUE (130 C3) *(🕮 J2)*

Visitors to this educational project can get a close look at the approximately 60 women weaving silk and buy the products they produce. Gallery and restaurant *(Budget)* with Khmer dishes *(it is advisable to book if you plan to eat: tel. 074 97 39 77 and 012 62 20 96). Mon–Sat 7.30–11.30am, 2–5pm, restaurant 7.30–10am | Sre Po Village | approx. 1.5 km east of the Sekong Bridge | www.mekongblue.com*

RAMSAR WETLANDS/MEKONG BOAT TRIPS ★ ● (130 C2–3) *(🕮 J2)*

After the end of the rainy season in October, a fascinating boat trip on the Mekong takes visitors through flooded forests such as those in the Ramsar Wetlands with herons, dazzlingly coloured kingfishers and myriads of fist-sized butterflies. It's well worth taking an excursion past traditional fishing settlements to the *Khone Phapheng Falls* (also: *Son Phammit*) near the border with Laos – stretching for some 14km (9mi) they are the widest in Asia. There are spectacular views from the ﹏ *Phnom Bong Khouy*, and homestays are possible in the village of *O Svay* near the border. The trip is made even more appealing by boat tours to see the freshwater dolphins near *Anlong Cheuteal*. The border crossing is near *Dom Kalor*, 55 km (34 mi) north of Stung Treng. You can charter a fishing boat at the pier in Sun Treng for a day's excursion – the price depends on your bargaining skills *(slow boat approx. 300,000 KHR)*. Homestay information: *tel. 074 97 38 58 | www.cepa-cambodia.org, www.ccben. org or Mr. Thea at the Riverside Guesthouse or Richie's Restaurant as well as www.mekongdiscoverytrail.com.* If you plan to enter Laos, be sure to get your visa beforehand!

The Mekong on the border to Laos is perfect for boat excursions

TRIPS & TOURS

The tours are marked in green in the road atlas,
pull-out map and on the back cover

① BATHING AND ISLAND HOPPING, SEAFOOD AND TEMPLE MOUNTAINS

Many Cambodians like to escape from the chaotic traffic in Phnom Penh at the weekend and head for the coast. But the south of Cambodia offers more than just bathing and island hopping; the provinces have many treasures waiting to be discovered: national parks in the jungle with wild animals and waterfalls, fishing villages and temple mountains. This 620 km (385 mi) tour in a hired car including a visit to the zoo, 'Dinosaur Park' and plenty of action is also suitable for families with children. You should plan on it taking one week.
Leaving **Phnom Penh → p. 40** drive to the southwest on the N 4 past rice fields and market villages, with views of the Cardamom Mountains in the distance. After you reach the village of Treng Trayeung 88km (55mi) further on, your driver should turn left and follow the road for 8km (5mi) to the Preah Suramarith Kossamak National Park, better known as the ⚊⚘ **Kirirom National Park**, with pine forests, waterfalls (such as the 30 m/100 ft high Chambok Cascade), bat caves and a pleasant climate at an altitude of around 700 m (2,300 ft) as well as environmentally friendly homestays *(tel. 012 29 28 76 and 023 35 72 30 in Phnom Penh | www.ccben. org and crdt.org.kh | Budget | admission 20,000 KHR).* The *Kirirom Hillside Resort* with comfortable log cabins and pool in a park with 'dinosaurs', ponies and kayaks waiting for you *(at the park entrance | tel.*

Photo: Beach near Sihanoukville

Excursions to experience the nature and culture of Cambodia – on the coast in the south or in the footsteps of the old rulers of Angkor in the north

016 59 09 99 | www.kiriromresort.com | *Moderate*) is an ideal starting point for exploring the park.

Back on the N4, after approx. 20 km (12 mi) you can stop to ask the ● INSIDER TIP female guardian spirit Ya Mao for her protection on the rest of your trip when you reach the Pich Nil Pass between the Cardamom and Elephant Mountains – all you have to do is light three joss sticks at one of the countless shrines and leave a 1,000 riel note in the donation box. The landscape now be- comes more tropical with coconut and sugar palms and oil-palm plantations. The right turn in Chamkar Luang takes you along a brand-new road to Koh Kong → p. 54 and Thailand; the left one to the lively seaside resort of Sihanoukville → p. 49, where you should spend at least two days relaxing on the beach or letting your hair down at the beach parties. On your way to the small riverside town of Kampot → p. 33, you will see the vast steep mountain wall of the Bokor Na- tional Park → p. 36, its plateau usually draped in clouds. There is also a fantastic view of Bokor from the ⚘ bungalows on the slope above the water in the drowsy seaside town of **Kep** → p. 37.

The N33 now heads towards **Takeo** (pop. 39,000) in the depths of the province and far off the beaten tourist track, across a pleasant landscape with rice fields, which are flooded during the rainy season, and a network of ancient canals (most attractive from July to October). Count on spending three hours here to take a chartered fishing boat *(80,000–105,000 KHR)* along *Canal number 15* and the *Stung Takeo* **INSIDER TIP** through the dazzling green rice fields, past people tending their ducks and buffalos, and fishing settlements until you reach the ruins of the temple at **Phnom Da** *(ca. 7,500 KHR)*. The temple has dominated the 100-m (330-ft) high hill of the same name and canals at its base since the 11th century and affords ⚘ fabulous panoramic view as far as Vietnam 10 km (6 mi) away. On your stopover to visit the small museum in **Angkor Borei** (pop. 14,000), you will discover many interesting facts about the harbour town and its importance as a trade centre during the period of the ancient Funan Khmer kingdom (1st–6th century); archaeologists even consider this area the birthplace of the Khmer civilisation. Today, around 10,000 of the total 15,000 Cambodian weaving women live in the Takeo region; many produce goods to be exported by the Cambodian Craft Cooperation *(www.silkfromcambodia.com)*. Most of the silk-weaving villages are near the N2 north of Takeo. The silk-weaving technique was probably introduced from India and China during the Funan period in the 2nd century and the exquisite goods produced sold to the nearby royal court from Takeo. The *Phnom Da Guesthouse* on the canal street *(tel. 016 82 60 83 | Budget)* is a good place to stay in Takeo.

The last day has come and you travel back to **Phnom Penh** along the N2 and past the temple mountain of ⚘ **Phnom**

An ancient network of canals runs through the countryside near Takeo

Chisor, which can be ascended via 500 steps *(25km/16mi to the north, 10,000 KHR)*; if you have children with you, you should definitely stop over at the vast **Phnom Tamao Zoological Garden** → p. 108. Temple fans can also visit the pretty ruins of **Ta Prohm** 30km (19mi) south of Phnom Penh; just as its namesake in Siem Reap, this was built by Jayavarman VII in the 13th century: prasat towers, Buddha statues and beautiful frescoes await you between colourful flowers, fortune tellers and musicians *(daily 7am–6pm | 10,000 KHR)*. It is then only a short walk to **Tonle Bati** with the wat of the same name – a popular lake for picnicking.

2 ON THE TRACES OF THE KHMER KINGS

Most tourists travel from Phnom Penh to Siem Reap and Angkor by bus. If you took the direct route along the N6 it would take less than six hours, but that would mean missing many fascinating attractions on the way such as the 1,300-year-old temple city of *Sambor Prei Kuk* and an almost 1,000-year-old bridge that is till intact. More remote ruins such as *Beng Mealea* are wonderful alternatives to the overrun ones in Angkor. The 580 km (360 mi) route, with some interesting detours to experience everyday rural life, will take two to three days.

The little centre of **Skun** (80 km/50 mi north of Phnom Penh) is the first, culinary interesting, stop: it is famous among the Khmer for its ● INSIDER TIP edible, fist-sized tarantulas *(bing)*. How about trying this exotic delicacy when you take a break at the motorway restaurant or at the main market? Fried crickets are another alternative… The *Skun Spider Sanctuary*, a breeding farm, has

500 steps lead up to the Phnom Chisor

an exhibition and garden where you can taste these specialities in unique combinations – such as chocolate-coated ants – as well as hearty crocodile and buffalo burgers *(1km north of the Skun roundabout | tel. 012 75 34 01)*.

It's worth spending the night in the *Khmer Village Homestay* with its simple, rustic, unique stilt huts *(tel. 012 63 57 18 | www.ccben.org | Budget | two days, all inclusive, approx. 150,000 KHR/person)* in the tiny village of **Baray** approx. 40km (25mi) to the north. It's also possible to take a ride on a bullock cart, see traditional dance shows and do volunteer work. There are several other attractions in the area around Baray including the **Santuk Silk Farm** with a tour that takes visitors from the mulberry trees via the various stages of production to the souvenir shop *(Mon–Sat 7–11am, 1–5pm | bookings tel. 012 90 66 04)*; the ☼ **Phnom Santuk** with the monastery of the same name at the top of a flight of 800(!) steps *(ca. 7,500 KHR)*; and the **Buddha Factory Village Kakaoh**, where you can watch the stonemasons at work and maybe even buy a shoulder-high Buddha for your terrace at home.

Some 35 km (22 mi) north of the town of **Kampong Thom** (pop. 66,000) you can visit the early Khmer temple of **Sambor Prei Kuk** *(information: www.samborpreikuk.com)*, which dates from the pre-Angkor era (7th century). The partly very bumpy N 64 takes you through traditional Khmer villages with stilt huts and bullock carts to the extensive temple complex in the middle of the forest. Sambor Prei Kuk, which was once the site of 100 temples, was erected by King Isanavarman I under the name of Isanapura – as the capital of the Asian kingdom of Chenla. The *Prasat Sambor*, the first of three building complexes, has copies of the figures of the gods Durga and Harihara in its brick towers (the originals are in Phnom Penh). Two stone lions watch over the *Prasat Tao*, the Lion Tower approx. 600 m to the southwest. Another impressive structure, around 600m to the southeast, is the *Prasat Yeai Poeun* with its central 30 m (100 ft) high tower sanctuary that was dedicated to Shiva; it is now partially in the clutches of gigantic trees *(daily 7am–5pm | 10,000 KHR | snack stands)*. In Kampong Thom, you can spend the night in small, but decent, balcony rooms in the *Arunras Hotel (tel. 062 96 12 94 | Budget)* or the more peaceful *Stung Sen Royal Garden (tel. 062 96 12 28 | Budget–Moderate)* on the riverside. The **INSIDER TIP** *Sambor Village Hotel* has an idyllic location with a small pool, attractive bungalows and restaurant on the Stung Sen *(19 rooms | tel. 062 96 13 91 | Moderate)*. Homestays are also possible in Kampong Thom and Sambor Prei Kuk *(information: www. ccben.org)*.

The figure of the god Harihara in the Prasat Sambor

In the middle of the Tonle Sap Basin – between marshland, rice fields and sugar palms – a massive arched bridge made of laterite blocks, the **INSIDER TIP** *Spean Prap Tos*, crosses the Stung Chikreng near the village of **Kampong Kdey** *(70 km/43 mi northwest of Kampong Thom)*. It was erected almost 100 years ago by Jayavarman VII and is decorated with mythical naga snakes winding their way along both sides. The two Angkor-era temples **INSIDER TIP** **Beng Mealea** and **INSIDER TIP** **Koh Ker**, which had

The bullock cart is still the main means of transport in rural areas

been mined for years, can be reached by turning right off the N7 in the hamlet of Dam Deik *(narrow road at the market, no signpost!)*. The two temple ruins are once again accessible now that the region has been demined. The area is notable for its idyllic, rural atmosphere; you will encounter farmers working in the rice fields, children on bullock carts, and monks in the village temples. **Beng Mealea** is 35 km (22 mi) away in the forest: the 12th-century temple is an amazing sight, its chaotically strewn stones providing an air of mystery similar to *Ta Prohm* in Angkor. Piles of rubble under the enormous roots of banyan trees, hidden galleries supported by columns that you can only reach by crawling on all fours through spider webs and over blocks of sandstone (there is an easier path over a wooden bridge, but then you won't feel like Indiana Jones). You will discover exquisite Shiva and Krishna reliefs, the apsaras look down at the few tourists from

hidden niches *(at the barrier a short distance before Beng Mealea | car approx. 10,000 KHR | admission to Beng Mealea 20,000 KHR | Koh Ker 40,000 KHR)*.

If you want to avoid the strenuous 70 km (43 mi) trip on a horrible gravel road from here to Koh Ker, especially in the rainy season, you can turn around – it's then only another 65 km (40 mi) from Beng Mealea to Siem Reap.

But real temple fans should definitely visit **Koh Ker**; above all, to see the more than 1,000-year-old *Prasat Thom*: unusually for Angkor architecture, the building rises up as an impressive 40-m (130-ft) high, seven-terraced, pyramid (unfortunately, it can not be climbed at the moment); in addition to this, are the scattered ruins of the tower, some bizarrely in the grip of roots, with impressive *lingas* in honour of Shiva *(danger of mines, do not leave the paths; there is also a simple guesthouse – Budget)*.

SPORTS & ACTIVITIES

Cambodia is a country that is ideal for adventurous, sporty types. Many kinds of sport, such as rock climbing and caving, are still in their infancy here, but the country's often untrammelled nature has enormous potential.

Motocross and mountain-bike tours with an off-road feeling on the dusty roads are very popular. The cooking courses and trekking tours in the national parks, which are becoming increasingly trendy, provide more fun than adrenalin rushes.

ANGKOR WAT HALF MARATHON

Thousands of runners from more than 40 countries congregate every December to take part in the *Angkor Wat Half Marathon (www.angkormarathon.org)*. Those who simply want to jog through Cambodian history past the temple ruins at least once in their life are probably better off going on the 5 km (3 mi) long *Fun Run*.

BICYCLE TOURS

Large sections of Cambodia are flat and there is not very much motorised traffic – this makes it ideal for cyclists. However, you still have to watch out: an increasing number of country roads are being surfaced and this has also led to an increase in accidents. The highlands pose a – still largely unexplored – challenge for mountain-bikers. It's possible to buy or hire basic bicycles in Phnom Penh; if you have higher sporting ambitions, you

Photo: Trekking in the Phnom Kulen National Park

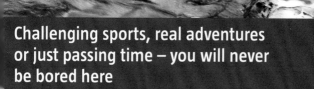

Challenging sports, real adventures or just passing time – you will never be bored here

should bring your own bike with you. *Buffalo Tours (www.buffalotours.com)* in Siem Reap organise interesting tours to less well-known parts of the country for average cyclists. *Pepy Ride (www.pepy ride.org)* makes it possible to combine your cycle tour with voluntary work.

BIRDWATCHING

Its many years of isolation caused by war and mining have made Cambodia an ideal refuge for many species of birds

threatened with extinction including the silver heron, grey pelican and osprey. In the dry season from December to March, the *Virachay National Park* near Siem Pang, Ratanakiri, the *Ramsar Wetlands* (Mekong) and *Prek Toal* (Tonle Sap Lake) are among the best areas for ornithologists to make their observations. In addition, there is the extensive marshland near Kampong Thom, the *Saurus Crane Conservation Area* near Ang Trapeang Thmor and *Tmatboey* near Preah Vihear with its many ibises *(homestays possi-*

ble | www.ccben.org). Information and tours: *Monsoon Tours (www.monsoontours.com)*, *Sam Veasna (www.samveasna.org)* and *Osmose (www.osmosetonlesap.net)* in Siem Reap. Internet: *www.vietnambirding.com*, *www.birdlifeindochina.org*

COOKING COURSES

Hobby cooks in the large tourist centres Phnom Penh, Siem Reap and Sihanoukville can start the day at the market, shopping for exotic vegetables, herbs and spices and then stir them around in a wok. Cooking lessons are available in Siem Reap – from *Le Tigre de Papier (www.letigredepapier.com)*, for example, or the more expensive *Cooks in Tuktuks (www.rivergarden.info)*. The *Frizz Restaurant* in Phnom Penh organises the *Cambodia Cooking Class (www.cambodia-cooking-class.com)* and the *Traditional Khmer Cookery School* is the place to learn the art of Khmer cuisine in Sihanoukville *(tel. 092 73 86 15 | half-day courses cost from approx. 45,000 KHR)*.

GOLF

Putting between the ruins: in Siem Reap, there are two courses to play; one of them, the Sofitel Hotel's demanding *Phokeethra Country Club*, incorporates the restored 11th-century Roluh Bridge *(www.phokeethragolf.com | 18 holes | green fees from approx. 265,000 KHR for guests)*. There are also two golf clubs near Phnom Penh: the nine-hole *Royal Cambodia Phnom Penh Golf Club (10km/6mi to the south of Phnom Penh)* and the luxurious *Cambodia Golf & Country Club*, the country's first 18-hole course, laid out between sugar palms and ponds *(35km/22mi southwest of Phnom Penh near the village of Kambol)*.

HIKING & TREKKING

Cambodia has approximately 20 national parks, conservation areas and biosphere reserves. The best infrastructure can be found in the *Virachay National Park* – some of the rangers speak English – where you will have a good chance of observing wild animals on the various

For those who don't want to paddle their own boat: cruises on the gigantic Tonle Sap Lake

adventure tours that are offered (www. yaklom.com). It is easy for tourists to reach the *Bokor National Park* and *Ream National Park* (with basic accommodation) from Sihanoukville, as well as the *Kirirom National Park* near Phnom Penh. The *Cardamom Mountains*, with the last surviving tigers and wild elephants, have great potential for the future.

KAYAK, CANOE & BOAT TOURS

The many rivers offer splendid opportunities for you to pick up your paddles and glide peacefully past fishing villages, pagodas and through jungle-like regions (*e.g. on the Tonle Sap Lake, near Battambang, Ratanakiri and on the coast near Sihanoukville and Kep; boats can be hired at the hotels or from specialist tour operators*). Even if you're not interested in being active yourself, boat tours on the Mekong (unfortunately, now only charter boots), on the Tonle Sap Lake and through the Mekong Delta as far as Vietnam are really worthwhile. For example, tours are offered between Phnom Penh

and Siem Reap (*www.cfmekong.com*). The luxurious river-cruise boat *Pandaw* sails back and forth between Saigon, Phnom Penh and Siem Reap (*www. pandaw.com*).

ROCK CLIMBING

The first rock climbers have arrived! It will not be long before the appropriate infrastructure becomes established as it has in the neighbouring countries Thailand and Vietnam. Until then: bring your own equipment! Among the areas with great potential for climbing are: the **INSIDER TIP** rugged karst hills near Kampot, Kampong Trach and Kampong Cham (with their own routes), Battambang in the north, as well as Takeo and Siem Reap. *Information: www.rockclimbingin cambodia.com*

SNORKELLING & DIVING

Several PADI diving schools in Sihanoukville offer dives and courses in English. Most of the diving areas are around 1.5 to 2 hours by boat away from the coast near the islands of Koh Kon, Koh Rong Samloem and Koh Tang where the underwater visibility is 10–25 m and sometimes up to 40 m. There, divers will come face to face with large schools of up-to-two-metre long Cobia perch, dazzling parrot fish and other colourful marine life. You will see blue-spotted stingrays, small (harmless) sharks and sometimes even dolphins if you go on a night dive. There are good diving areas to the west of Koh Kong, particularly in the Koh Sdach Archipelago with its intact banks of coral. The best season for diving is from November to approx. May; the sea is often too rough in the rainy season. *Information: Scuba Nation (www.dive cambodia.com).*

TRAVEL WITH KIDS

At first glance, Cambodia might not seem like the best place to travel with children, if only for reasons of health and hygiene (on account of typhoid, hepatitis, malaria, dengue, etc; don't forget to take all the necessary precautions with the appropriate vaccinations, mosquito repellent, and so on!) While travelling, make sure that the entire family uses a sunscreen with high protection factor, that everyone wears a hat or cap and drinks a lot of liquid! You can enjoy the cola, chips and spaghetti in the tourist centres but you should forget about ice cream in Cambodia. Most of the hotels do not have special beds for children and napkins are also rare (pack enough cloth napkins and dummies).

The individual chapters list classic activities that children of all ages enjoy: elephant rides in the provinces of Mondulkiri and Ratanakiri, or frolicking in the sea at the coast in Sihanoukville and other resorts.

KAMPOT

TEOK CHHOU

The small Teok Chhou Zoo near Kampot is definitely worth a stopover. *Daily 7am–6pm | entrance fee 15,000 KHR | 8km (5mi) north of Kampot*

PHNOM PENH

CHILDREN'S LIBRARY AND CINEMA

Cartoons for children are shown regularly at the *Institut Français Cambodge (French Cultural Center)*; there are comic exhibitions, Khmer pop and rap concerts, and a children's library in the Media Centre – parents can attend lectures and courses or while away the time in the garden café *Mit Samlanh (daily 7am–9pm)* over café au lait and croissants. *218 Street 184 | tel. 023 72 13 82 | www.ccf-cambodge.org*

PHNOM TAMAO ZOOLOGICAL GARDEN AND WILDLIFE RESCUE CENTER

This is the best and largest zoo in the country. It is also where many illegally caught animals have found a new home. Black bears, deer, tigers and elephants live in the cages and enclosures here and it is even possible to go into some of them – the gibbons provide the most action. *Daily 8am–4pm | 20,000 KHR, children approx. 7,500 KHR | 44km (27mi) south of Phnom Penh*

Butterflies and ponies, shadow puppets and cartoons – children can have a lot of fun in Cambodia

PHNOM PENH WATER PARK

Pools with waves and gigantic waterslides (only at the weekend); during the week, fountains and huge rubber rings: to sum it up – there is no end to the fun and games in the Water Park in Phnom Penh (its security and maintenance however do not meet European standards). *Daily 9.30am–5.30 pm (less full on weekdays 10am–2pm) | 10,000 KHR on weekdays, 15,000 KHR at the weekend | 50 Pochentong Road, towards the airport*

SIEM REAP

BUTTERFLY GARDEN RESTAURANT

1,500 butterflies in a tropical garden (under netting). While their parents listen to traditional live music or enjoy an aromatic footbath *(in the happy hour from 3–7pm)*, the children can be entertained by something completely different: every Mon, Thu and Sat hundreds of butterflies, caught by children from poor villages who are paid for their work, are set free at 11am. *9am–10pm | between the river and Wat Bo St., near the Wat Prohm Rot Bridge | www.butterfliesofangkor.com | Budget*

THE HAPPY RANCH

You can book riding lessons on Cambodian ponies at Sary Pann's horse ranch near Siem Reap *(1 hour from 75,000 KHR)*, go on horseback or lengthy carriage rides to the temples in the surroundings. *N6 towards the airport, 1.5km west of Siem Reap | tel. 012 92 00 02 | www.thehappyranch.com*

SHADOW PUPPET THEATRE

The *sbeik thom* and *sbeik touch* (also: *sbeik toot*) shadow-puppet plays, as well as traditional dances, are performed by children from the Krousar Thmey Orphanage in the *La Noria Hotel* in Siem Reap. *Wed and Sun 7.30pm | approx. 20,000 KHR plus extra price for dinner | tel. 063 96 42 42 | www.lanoriaangkor.com*

FESTIVALS & EVENTS

OFFICIAL HOLIDAYS

1 Jan New Year's Day; **7 Jan** Cambodia's liberation from the Khmer Rouge by the Vietnamese; **in Feb** *Meak Bochea* (Buddhist full-moon celebration); **8 March** International Women's Day; **1 May** Labour Day; **in May** *Visaka Bochea* (Birth, Enlightenment and Death of Buddha); **13–15 May** King Norodom Sihamoni's birthday; **18 June** Queen Norodom Monineath Sihanouk's birthday; **in Sept** *Bon Phchom Ben* (ancestral celebration); **24 Sept** Constitution Day; **29 Oct** Coronation Day; **31 Oct** King Norodom Sihanouk's birthday (the 'King-Father of Cambodia'); **9 Nov** National Holiday (Independence Day); **10 Dec** International Day of Human Rights

CAMBODIAN FESTIVALS

APRIL

Things almost get out of hand in Cambodia when the Khmer celebrate the New Year ▶ *Bonn Choul Chham Thmey* for at least three days at the end of the harvest period in mid-April (from 13/14): on country roads, in the hotels (the room prices double, book early!) and restaurants (either full or closed). The pagodas

appear to almost burst at the seams with all the festively dressed visitors on New Year's Day: they dance the ▶ *ram vong*, a kind of slow-motion line dance, and bring offerings to the monks and Buddha – in small banana-leaf baskets full of money, food, joss sticks, tobacco, flowers and fruit. Lucky numbers play a big role in this: one donates five candles, seven cigarettes and so on... To show their gratitude, the monks then pour buckets of holy water over the faithful. This is because the New Year is the time for a thorough (symbolic) purification: Buddha statues and houses are cleaned and the people buy new clothes. If you're driving along the country roads at this time, you will see more-or-less tipsy 'highwaymen' who – dancing, laughing and singing – block the road and beg for 'donations'.

MAY

The square in front of the National Museum is symbolically ploughed as part of the ▶ *Bon Chroat Preah Nongkoal*, the Royal Ploughing Ceremony, when sowing time starts at the beginning of the monsoon period in May. The Royal Ploughing Ceremony is a kind of weather forecast and prophecy carried out by as-

Cheerful festivals, royal ceremonies and oxen as oracles – join in celebrating Cambodian holidays

trologists and the royal oxen: after ploughing, the oxen can choose from rice, maize, beans, grass and other field crops, as well as water and wine, set before them in gold bowls – whatever they eat will do especially well the coming season; if the oxen drink the wine, however, the farmers and all of Cambodia will face a catastrophic year, possibly with flooding. No matter how the omen turns out: this typical form of popular superstition is a colourful event with many people in traditional dress taking part.

OCTOBER/NOVEMBER

Thousands gather on the banks of the Tonle Sap in Phnom Penh to celebrate the end of the rainy season in the three-day full-moon 'festival of the changing currents', the largest in the country, with spectacular boat regattas, magnificently illuminated ships and fireworks. The background of the ▶ ★ ● **Bon Om Touk** lies in the reversal of the flow of the cur-

rent in the Tonle Sap River when it is no longer able to contain the masses of water that have swollen the Mekong and flows backwards into the Tonle Sap Lake. In the old days, the god-like Khmer kings raised their hand to 'order' the river to change its direction. Since the 1990s, following decades of civil war, genocide and Communist occupation, the king once again takes his place on the VIP stand where the Mekong and Tonle Sap meet. One of his royal boats 'cuts' the rope stretched across the river, the symbolic gateway through which the Tonle Sap is once again permitted to flow towards the sea – with millions upon millions of fish. If you are lucky, you will witness this miracle of nature – or at least see some sure signs of it: in the morning, the bows of the fishing boats point in a different direction than the night before, and the water hyacinths float upstream instead of down.

LINKS, BLOGS, APPS & MORE

LINKS

▶ www.world-heritage-tour.org/asia/southeast-asia/khmer-empire/map.html Beam yourself into the Khmer Empire! The interactive panoramic photographs make it possible for you to stand in the middle of the mountains of rubble at Preah Khan and Preah Vihear

▶ www.bongthom.com/akonline/selectchapterek.asp Here, you will find language training in Khmer to ensure that your Cambodian isn't gibberish (in English)

▶ www.khmernetradio.com Prepare yourself for the Cambodian music you will hear as soon as you enter one of the typical country inns. Weird and wonderful oldies and Ram Vong classics on the Khun Pimoj Radio Network

BLOGS & FORUMS

▶ andybrouwer.co.uk/ctales1.html Andy Brouwer has travelled through Cambodia since 1994 and lived and worked in Phnom Penh since 2007. He now feeds his English-language blog 'Cambodian Tales' with well-researched travel reports from all corners of the country and other interesting articles – a real insider

▶ livinginpp.wordpress.com Freddy, a Swiss nomad, has reported on Cambodia, Vietnam and Laos – in English – since 2009: on his travels, the bars and restaurants he has visited, corruption, the weather and much much more...

▶ blueladyblog.com The blogger Kounila Keo has research films and excerpts from feature films on her English-language site

▶ loungung.com Loung Ung, the well known authoress and activist against landmines, collects all kinds of interesting news on her English-language website – from edible tarantulas, over rock bands to the Khmer Rouge tribunal

Regardless of whether you are still preparing your trip or already in Cambodia: these addresses will provide you with more information, videos and networks to make your holiday even more enjoyable

VIDEOS & STREAMS

▶ www.cambodiatribunal.org This makes it possible to follow the proceedings of the genocide tribunal in the courtroom in Phnom Penh (with English subtitles)

▶ www.youtube.com/watch?v=ESUdB6mVIaO Angelina Jolie talks about her first filming in Cambodia in the year 2000 and how the country changed her. The whole thing is actually 'only' a charity advertising vehicle for Louis Vuitton bags – but shot magnificently by star photographer Leibovitz in Cambodia

APPS

▶ World Nomads Cambodian Language Guide Never be at a loss for words! This English-language app list the most important terms for travellers with the appropriate translations – and a short language course

▶ Cambodia Wallpapers Would you like to have Cambodia with you wherever you are? All you need to do is download this app with beautiful photos of the country onto your Smartphone

NETWORKS

▶ www.couchsurfing.org Get to know a completely different side of Cambodia. You will be able to find a place to sleep with people who actually live where others go for a holiday over this website

▶ www.tripwolf.com Here, travellers give fellow travellers tips. Enter 'Cambodia' into the search field. Many photos from community members

▶ www.cambodia.com.au/photo/albums/cambodia-photography-club Magnificent photographs of Cambodia and the Cambodians can be admired on the website of the Cambodia Photo Club

TRAVEL TIPS

ARRIVAL

✈ There are no direct flights from the UK to Cambodia. *Malaysia Airlines* flies from London to Kuala Lumpur and, from there, on to Phnom Penh *(www.malaysiaairlines.com)*. *AirFrance* flies from London to Paris where you change for the flights to Phnom Penh *(www.airfrance.co.uk)*. *Thai Airways* make the journey via Bangkok *(www.thaiairways.com)*; flying time is approx. 13–14 hours, air fare approx. 800 pounds. There are indirect flights from the USA with KLM *(www.klm.com)*, AirFrance and Singapore Airlines *(www.singaporeair.com)*, fare approx. 1,200 dollars.

ARRIVAL & DEPARTURE

The four-week *Visa on arrival* is issued when you enter the country at the airport in Phnom Penh and Siem Reap for 20 US dollars, a passport photo and a passport that is valid for at least six months; this also applies to the border crossings with Thailand, Vietnam and Laos. Information (and electronic visa): *www.immigration.gov.kh* and *www.cambodia-airports.com*. Electronic visas can only be applied for online a maximum of two weeks before the start of the trip; the process takes 3–5 days (20 + 5 US dollars) and they are valid for a maximum of 30 days, single entry and not at all border crossings in the country. Information: *www.mfaic.gov.kh/evisa*. The Cambodian government has issued a warning about the following unauthorised websites offering electronic visas: *www.cambodiaonarrival.com, www.cambodia-evisa.com, www.welovecambodia.com*. The most popular land borders from Thailand include: *Aranyaprathet/Poipet (to Siem Reap)* and *Hat Lek/Cham Yeam (Koh Kong, Sihanoukville)* on the coast; from Vietnam: *Moc Bai/Bavet, Svay Rieng (Phnom Penh)* and *Xa Xia/Prek Chak (Kep; not with an electronic visa!)*; from Laos: *Veun Kham/Dong Kralor on the upper Mekong (Stung Treng);* all with a Cambodian *Visa on arrival* for 20 US dollars; have a passport photo with you – a new one costs no more than 2 US dollars – as of late, fingerprints have also been taken. There are no additional 'stamp taxes' etc. The visa procedure at the border is uncomplicated and usually over in a few minutes. However, there have been an increasing number of fraud attempts made by some Cambodian officials (e.g. 5 US dollars or 100 baht as a handling charge, 30 US dollars or 1,000 baht for the visa instead of the 20 US dollars displayed on the official notice board).
The border crossings from and to Thailand (*Poipet/Aranyaprathet* and *Koh*

RESPONSIBLE TRAVEL

It doesn't take a lot to be environmentally friendly whilst travelling. Don't just think about your carbon footprint whilst flying to and from your holiday destination but also about how you can protect nature and culture abroad. As a tourist it is especially important to respect nature, look out for local products, cycle instead of driving, save water and much more. If you would like to find out more about eco-tourism please visit: *www.ecotourism.org*

From arrival to weather

Holiday from start to finish: the most important addresses and information for your trip to Cambodia

Kong on the coast) are especially notorious. Cheap Thai (bus) tourist operators also play along and make their passengers get off somewhere before the border or in front of a travel agency. The best thing to do is either fly or apply online for an E-visa. If not – remember, when you get to the border, keep smiling, have yourself driven straight to the *Immigration Office*, preferably before noon, queue up at the *Non-Thai Nationals* counter, only pay in US dollars, and if you have suspicions ask for an official receipt. Once you leave the visa hut in Poipet you walk through no-man's-land. It is not necessary to exchange money; you can pay for everything at the border crossing in US dollars or baht. Have yourself driven straight to the bus terminus (e.g. with the – really free – shuttle bus to the *Poipet station for buses to Angkor*) and buy your onward ticket there from the bus-service operator. If you intend to travel on to Laos or Vietnam by road or water, you should have the appropriate visas beforehand. International departures by air: the 25 US dollar departure tax has been included in the ticket price since April 2011.

BANKS & MONEY

Banks are usually open Mon–Fri 8am–3.30/4pm; some also Sat 8–11.30am/noon. The riel is Cambodia's official currency but the US dollar is commonly used to pay for anything more expensive than a bowl of noodle soup. You should have a mix of a few thousand riels and some dollars with you in cash, as well as US dollar traveller's cheques (2–4 percent) and your credit/debit card (cash dispensers in Phnom Penh, Siem Reap, Sihanoukville, Battambang, Kampot and Sen Monorom). The major hotels accept the usual credit cards. It is often more profitable to exchange money at licensed *Money Change* offices; they can be found everywhere in the country – often in nondescript stands.

CLIMATE, WHEN TO GO

Cambodia has a tropical monsoon climate characterised by a rainy season from April/

CURRENCY CONVERTER

£	KHR	KHR	£
1	6,500	5,000	0.77
3	19,000	10,000	1.55
5	32,000	25,000	3.88
13	84,000	50,000	7.75
40	258,000	80,000	12.40
75	484,000	150,000	23
120	775,000	500,000	78
250	1,610000	1,200000	186
500	3,230000	10,000000	1550

$	KHR	KHR	$
1	4,000	5,000	1.23
3	12,000	10,000	2.46
5	20,000	25,000	6.16
13	52,000	50,000	12.33
40	160,000	80,000	20
75	300,000	150,000	37
120	488,000	500,000	123
250	1,015000	1,200000	296
500	2,030000	10,000000	2,470

For current exchange rates see www.xe.com

May to October with short, but heavy, downpours. The best time to travel is during the cooler dry season from November/December to February/March with temperatures around 28 °C (82 °F); it can cool down to only a few degrees above freezing in the mountains (Mondulkiri). The hottest month is October – up to 38 °C (100 °F) and the rainiest is October.

CONSULATES & EMBASSIES

UK EMBASSY

27–29 Street 75 | Sangkat Srah Chak | Khan Daun Penh | Phnom Penh | tel. 023 427124 | http://ukincambodia.fco.gov.uk

US EMBASSY

#1, Street 96 | Sangkat Wat Phnom | Khan Daun Penh | Phnom Penh | tel. 023 728000 | http://cambodia.usembassy.gov

CUSTOMS

The import or export of foreign currency amounting to more than US$ 10,000 must be declared. There are no additional restrictions; as a rule it is permitted to bring up to 1.5 litres of spirits and 10 packets of cigarettes into the country. It is forbidden to export antiques (except with an export permit from the Fine Arts Department in Phnom Penh, organised by the dealer) and cultural assets such as sandstone reliefs. The following articles may be imported into the EU duty-free: 200 cigarettes or 50 cigars or 250 grams of tobacco, 1 litre of spirits above – or 2 litres below – 22 percent, other goods such as coffee, tea, perfume and presents up to a total value of 2,150,000 KHR.

ELECTRICITY

220 volt, an adapter is sometimes necessary; the frequent blackouts make it a good idea to have a pocket torch with you.

HEALTH

Get advice from an Institute for Tropical Medicine as soon as possible! It is advisable to have (booster) vaccinations against polio, tetanus, diphtheria, typhoid, as well as hepatitis A (if necessary, B) and rabies. With the exception of Phnom Penh, Cambodia is considered a malaria and dengue region (there is also dengue in Phnom Penh). Anti-malaria tablets have become increasingly ineffective as a result of resistance and it is therefore necessary to resort to other forms of mosquito protection: wear long-sleeved, light-coloured clothing from dusk to dawn, use a protective lotion and mosquito coils and nets and be sure to have emergency medicine (the best is Malarone) with you. Some rules about eating: no ice cream, unpeeled fruit, salad and raw vegetables, as well as tap water that has not been boiled, and only use cylindrically-shaped ice cubes (produced commercially). The medical facili-

BUDGETING

Noodle soup	approx. 0.40–0.80 £ / 0.60–1.20 $	for a serving
Angkor Beer	approx. 0.80 £ / 1.20 $	for a bottle
Massage	5–15 £ / 7–22 $	for one hour
Shawl	0.40 £ / 0.60 $	for a krama shawl
Cyclo	approx. 3–6 £ / 5–9 $	for a one-day tour in Phnom Penh
Internet	0.40–3 £ / 0.50–5 $	for one hour

ties in the chemists and hospitals are inadequate (with the exception of the international SOS Clinics in Phnom Penh and Siem Reap). A fully equipped first-aid kit (with sterile single-use syringes) is essential. In the case of a serious sickness, you should fly out to Bangkok or Singapore as soon as possible. And, do not forget to take out international health insurance including the option of emergency transport back home.

INFORMATION

ASIAN TRAILS
22 Street 249 | Phnom Penh | tel. 023 21 65 55 | www.asiantrails.info

ICS TRAVEL GROUP (OFFICIAL CAMBODIAN TOURIST OFFICE)
870 Market Street, Suite 923 | San Francisco, CA 94102, USA | tel. 0415 4 34 40 15 | www.indochina-services.com

LOCAL ADVENTURES
c/o Lotus Lodge | Siem Reap | tel. 063 96 61 40 | tel. in Phnom Penh: 023 99 04 60 | www.local-adventures.com

MONSOON TOURS
Siem Reap Office: 030 Phnom Steng Thmey (Svay Donkom district) | tel. 063 96 66 56, office in Phnom Penh: 27 Street 351 | Sangkat Boeng Kak 1 (Tuol Kork district) | tel. 023 96 96 16 | www.monsoon-tours.com

INTERNET

www.tourismcambodia.com: comprehensive information on travel in Cambodia.
www.stay-another-day.org: action group for responsible tourism.
www.childsafe-cambodia.org is a child-welfare organisation devoted to protecting minors in tourist destinations.

PERSONAL SAFETY

The political situation is relatively stable; at the time of going to press, the only border conflict was in the area near Preah Vihear. Avoid any demonstrations and political events. The country roads and the Mekong are now considered safe. The number of pickpocketing and robbery offences on lonely beaches is increasing in Phnom Penh und Sihanoukville. Always keep your bags in front of you on a cyclo, tuktuk or moped-taxi and at markets and festivals in Phnom Penh. On no account should you leave the marked paths in remote regions around Battambang and Pailin, temples such as Preah Vihear, Phnom Kulen and Koh Ker, as well as in the national parks (danger of mines). Riding a motor bike is the most dangerous means of transport (never without a helmet!) and the number of road deaths is rapidly increasing in Cambodia.

Village life far away from Phnom Penh

PHONE & MOBILE PHONE

International dialling code for Cambodia: 00855; dialling code from Cambodia to the UK: 001-44; to the USA: 001-01.

FROM CAMBODIA
The easiest way to make international calls is from hotels *(10,000–20,000 KHR/min)* or post offices *(ca. 7,500 KHR/min)*. There

are also prepaid phonecards *(for 20,000–200,000 KHR, approx. 3,650 KHR/min, MPTC and Camintel are the cheapest)*. It is more economical to use the dialling codes 177-44 und 007-44 *(ca. 1,500 KHR/min)*. As a rule, the cheapest way to telephone is from Internet shops *(ca. 150–1,500 KHR)*.

MOBILE PHONES

Cambodian SIM cards *(for 25,000–45,000 KHR, plus prepaid cards from 20,000 KHR, e.g. Camshin)* or VOIP dialling codes (e.g. 177-44, 165-44), with which calls can be made to the UK for 250–1,000 KHR/min, are cheaper than using your own mobile phone. However, you will need an unlock code and newly assigned telephone num- ber. Used mobile phones can be purchased very inexpensively or hired at some loca- tions (e.g. at the Pochentong Airport). *In- formation: www.camintel.com, www.mptc. gov.kh, www.mfone.com.kh.*

PHOTOGRAPHY

It is advisable to bring batteries and memory cards with you. Be cautious about photographing soldiers and mili- tary installations. It is polite to ask for permission before taking pictures, espe- cially of monks, highland tribespeople and religious ceremonies – if somebody shakes his head or makes any other ges- ture rejecting your request, respect it!

WEATHER IN PHNOM PENH

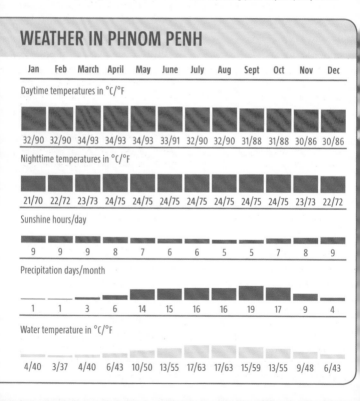

	Jan	Feb	March	April	May	June	July	Aug	Sept	Oct	Nov	Dec
Daytime temperatures in °C/°F												
	32/90	32/90	34/93	34/93	34/93	33/91	32/90	32/90	31/88	31/88	30/86	30/86
Nighttime temperatures in °C/°F												
	21/70	22/72	23/73	24/75	24/75	24/75	24/75	24/75	24/75	24/75	23/73	22/72
Sunshine hours/day												
	9	9	9	8	7	6	6	5	5	7	8	9
Precipitation days/month												
	1	1	3	6	14	15	16	16	19	17	9	4
Water temperature in °C/°F												
	4/40	3/37	4/40	6/43	10/50	13/55	17/63	17/63	15/59	13/55	9/48	6/43

PUBLIC TRANSPORT

BUSES

Coaches and mini-buses (the latter cannot really be recommended) depart daily from Phnom Penh for all areas of the country and even across the border – the buses operated by *Mekong Express (tel. 023 42 75 18)* are the best. Tickets can be purchased in the guesthouses and in the offices on the Riverside Promenade in Phnom Penh; for example, those on Street 104. We advise against the new Siem Reap-Sihanoukville overnight buses (10–11 hours travel time, high accident rate).

PLANE

There are flights between Phnom Penh and Siem Reap, as well as between Sihanoukville and Siem Reap.

HIRE CARS

It is only possible to hire a car with a driver; approx. 90,000–145,000 KHR/day in the cities and from around 180,000 KHR/day in the provinces depending on the destination and road conditions.

FERRIES AND HIGH-SPEED BOATS

Only high-speed, extremely noisy, boats that travel at a breakneck speed and can be rather dangerous transport passengers on the Mekong these days. There are also express boats from Phnom Penh across the Tonle Sap Lake to Siem Reap *(5–7 hours, hardly recommendable)*. The landscape makes the boat trip from Siem Reap to Battambang much more rewarding. Boats travel several times daily on the beautiful stretch from Phnom Penh through the Mekong Delta over the border to Vietnam *(Chau Doc) (ca. 75,000 KHR)*. It is more expensive to take the *Victoria Sprite* operated by the Victoria Hotels to Chau Doc *(www.victoria hotels-asia.com | get a visa for Vietnam beforehand!)* Further information p. 107.

TAXI, MOPED-TAXI, TUKTUK, CYCLO

Taxis are available in Phnom Penh and Siem Reap (usually without a taximeter; ask the hotel receptions for the price or bargain with the driver). You should not take a moped-taxi in the chaotic traffic of Phnom Penh (if you do, wear a helmet – it is obligatory!) but a safer tuktuk or three-wheel cyclo (agree on the fare before you start; usually 1.50–2 US dollars per stretch). You should be able to hire a bicycle for less than 5,000 KHR a day; for a moped (officially forbidden) the cost is about 20,000 KHR.

TIME

There is a plus seven-hour time difference in winter; this is reduced to plus six hours during European daylight saving time.

TIPPING

It is customary to tip tour guides, drivers, waiters and room service. You can give money to handicapped beggars (often mine victims) but it is better not to do this with children as they will then not go to school and also because their begging is often organised. A small donation placed in the containers provided is a matter of course after temple ceremonies (in all cases: approx. 750 KHR – always bear in mind that the average monthly salary is only approx. 150,000 KHR).

WHAT TO WEAR

The most suitable clothing is knee-length trousers or skirts, of light cotton or linen material, for temple visits, a pullover, socks for trips to the mountains, a rain cape, sunhat, sports shoes or trekking sandals; for women: a sarong or shorts so that they can bathe 'decently' in rivers and under waterfalls in the company of the (conservative) locals.

USEFUL PHRASES KHMER

PRONUNCIATION

For pronunciation, all the Khmer words have been assigned a simple transliteration (in square brackets).

IN BRIEF

Yes/No/ (masculine form)	ហាទ [baht]/ទេ [day]
Yes/No/ (Feminine form)	ចា [jaah]/ទេ [day]
Maybe	ប្រហែល [prohrhail]
Please/You're welcome!	សូមអញ្ជើញ [soum unjuhn]
Thank you	អរគុណ [aw khun]
Excuse me, please!	សូមអភ័យទោស! [soum toh]
Pardon?	អត់ទោស? [odtohk]
I understand/	ខ្ញុំយល់ [knyom yuall]/
I don't understand	ខ្ញុំយមិនយល់ទេ [knyom men yuall day]
Could you please help me?	តើលោកអាចជួយខ្ញុំបានរយោធទ? [dahl lok at khoo-ee knyom ban royoh day]
I would like to …/	ខ្ញុំចង់ [knyom khom ban]/
I wouldn't like to …/	ខ្ញុំអត់ចង់ [knyom ot khom ban day]
I like this/	ខ្ញុំពេញចិត្ត [knyom bing khet]/
I don't like this	ខ្ញុំមិនពេញចិត្តទេ [knyom men bing khet day]
have you got …?	តើលោកមាន? [dahl lok meh-an]
How much is it?	តើថ្លៃប៉ុន្មាន? [dahl thlay bun mann]
What time is it?	តើម៉ោងប៉ុន្មានហើយ? [dahl maong bun mann hai]

GREETINGS, FAREWELL

Good morning!/	សួស្ដី! [suosday]/
Good evening!	រាត្រីសួស្ដី! [reh-a trai suosday]
Hello!/	ជំរាបសួរ! [johm riab sua]/
Good bye!	ជំរាបលា! [johm riab layer]
See you!	
(to an …)	
… older/younger man	លោកប្រុស [lawk bros]/ឪនប្រុស [boh ohn bros]
… older/younger woman	អ្នកស្រី [nairk sray]/ឪនស្រី [boh ohn sray]
How are you [doing]?	តើលោកសុខសប្បាយជាទេ? [dahl lawk sok sabai jeea day]

លោកចេះនិយាយភាសាខ្មែរឬទេ?

'Do you speak Khmer?' This guide will help you to say the basic words and phrases in Khmer.

My name is ...	ខ្ញុំឈ្មោះ [knyom chmoh]
Nice to meet you!	ខ្ញុំរីករាយណាស់ដែលហានស្គាល់លោក! [knyom rayk reh-ai nahk dail ban skawl lawk]
Goodbye!	ខ្ញុំលាសិនហើយ! [knyom layer sen hai]
See you later!	ជួបគ្នាបន្តិចទៀត! [khup kneh-ar bon text teh-at]

TRAVEL

left/right	ឆ្វេង [chwayng]/ស្ដាំ [sdum]
straight ahead	ត្រង់ [trang]
close/far	ទៅកាន់ [doh kahn]/ឆ្ងាយ [chngai]
Please, where is ...?	សូមអភ័យទោស តើ ... នៅទីណា? [som apai took dahl ... noh dee nah]
Main station	ស្ថានីយចតផ្លើង [satanee rotployng]
Airport	ព្រលានយន្តហោះ [broh lay-an yohnhoh]
Hotel	សណ្ឋាគារ [son tah keh-ar]
I would like to rent ...	ខ្ញុំចង់ជួល... [knyom khang khul ...]
Bicycle	កង់ [kong]
Taxi	តាក់ស៊ី [taxee]
How far?	តើចំងាយប៉ុន្មានដែល? [dahl khomgai bun mann dail]
Accident	គ្រោះថ្នាក់ [kroo tanak]
Help!	ជួយផង! [choo-ee pang]
Attention!/ Caution!	សេចក្ដីប្រយ័ត្ន [satkdai prohyat]/ ប្រុងប្រយ័ត្ន [prog prohyat]
Please call ...	សូមលោកហៅ ... អោយលឿន [som lawk hao ... aov lurn]
... a doctor	គ្រូពេទ្យ [kroh peht]
... an ambulance	ឡានពេទ្យ [lahn peht]
... the police	ប៉ូលិស [lahn police]
... the fire brigade	ឡានទឹក [lahn toyg]
Do you have a first-aid kit?	តើលោកមានបដាប់រំរបស? [dahl lawk meh-an brohdab rom robohs]
It was my/your fault	នេះគឺជាកំហុសរបស់ខ្ញុំ [nikh keh-ah kom hohroboh knyom]/ របស់លោក [roboh lawk]
Please give me your name and address	សូមលោកប្រគល់មកខ្ញុំ ឈ្មោះរបស់លោកនិង អស័យដ្ឋានរបស់លោក [som lawk broh kuol mok knyom chmho robos lawk noyg asayatan robos lawk]

FOOD & DRINK

Where is there a good restaurant?	តើទីនេះមាន ភាគនីយដ្ឋានល្អរឺទេ? [dahl dee nikh meh-an pokhaneeyatan lah-or dail royoh day]
Could you please book a table for tonight for four?	សូមលោកទុកបំរុងសំរាប់យើងពេលល្ងាចនេះ កុម្ភយសំរាប់គ្នាបួននាក់ [som lawk dook bom rong som-ramb yoy bel lagneh-arg nikh dok muoy somramb kneh-ar bun neh-ak]
Your health!/Cheers!	ដើម្បីសុខភាពរបស់លោកអ្នក! [doymbay sokhapeh-ap robos lawk neh-ak]
The food is very good	ម្ហូបនេះឆ្ងាញ់ណាស់ [mahohm nikh chnang nas]
May I have the bill, please	សូមមេគ្គាគិតលុយ [som mehta keh-at loy]

SHOPPING

Where can I find ...?	តើទីណាខ្ញុំរកឃើញ? [dahl deenna knyom rok khehung]
Pharmacy / chemist	ឧសថស្ថាន/ហ្វាម៉ាសី [pharmacee]
Bakery	ហាងលក់នំបុ័ង [hang lawk noom bang]
Grocery	ហាងលក់ម្ហូបអាហា [hang lohk mahomb aha]
Department store	ហាងលក់ទំនិញ [hang lawk toom ning]
Market	ផ្សារ [psar]
When does the department store open/close?	តើហាងលក់ទំនិញបិទបើកពេលណា? [dahl hang lohk toom ning bat tweh-ar beh-ana]
How much is ...?	តើរបស់នេះតៃម្លៃប៉ុន្មាន? [dahl robos nikh tley bun mann]

ACCOMMODATION

Could you please recommend ...?	តើលោកអាចប្រាប់ខ្ញុំ? [dahl lawk art prap knyom]
... a hotel	សណ្ឋាគា [son ta geea]
... a pension	ផ្ទះសំណាក់ [ptehr somnak]
Do you have any ... left?	តើលោកនៅមាន ...? [dahl lawk noh meh-an]
single room	បន្ទប់មួយទំនៃរឺទេ [pontoob muoy tomnay royoh day]
double room	បន្ទប់មួយគ្រពីរទៃនៃរឺទេ [baan toop muoy kray pee tomnay royoh day]
one night	សំរាប់មួយយោប [somrab muoy yohb]
one week	សំរាប់មួយសប្ដាហ៍ [somrab muoy sabada]
How much is this room?	តើបន្ទប់នេះតំលៃប៉ុន្មាន? [dahl pontoob nikh domlay bun mann]
shower/sit-down bath	ជាមួយបន្ទប់ទឹក [kheh-a muoy baan toop dek]
breakfast	ជាមួយស្រុសស្រួបបាលេព្រឹក [kheh-a muoy srossrob beprek]
half board	ជាមួយស្រុសស្រួបពេលព្រឹកនឹងពេលថ្ងៃត្រង់ [kheh-a muoy srossrob behtgaitrong]

HEALTH

doctor	គ្រូពេទ្យ [krow peht]
Can you recommend a doctor?	តើលោកអាចរកគ្រូពេទ្យអោយខ្ញុំបានទេ? [dahl lawk art rok krow peht ao-ee knyom ban royoh day]
Ich habe ...	ខ្ញុំ [knyom]
... fever/... diarrhoea	គ្រុនក្ដៅ [kdao krun]/ចុះរាក [kho ree-uk]
... headache/... toothache	ឈឺក្បាល [khoyv kbal]/ឈឺធ្មេញ [khoyv tming]

BANKS, MONEY

Bank	ធនាគារ [tor neea geea]
Could you tell me where ...	លោកអាចប្រាប់ខ្ញុំបានទេ? [dahl lawk art prab knyom ban royoh day]
... there's a bank?	... តើធនាគារនៅទីណា? [dahl tor neea geea noh deena]
... there's a bureau de change?	... តើកន្លែងដូរប្រាក់នៅទីណា? [dahl kontlay dohprak noh deena]

POST

Post	ប្រៃសណីយ៍ [praysanee]
How much is ...?	តើតំលៃប៉ុន្មាន? [dahl domlay bun mann]
... a letter	សំបុត្រមួយ [sombot muoy]
... a postcard	កាតមួយ [kat muoy]

NUMBERS

0	សូន្យ [soun]	18	ដប់ប្រាំបី [dorb pram bay]
1	មួយ [muoy]	19	ដប់ប្រាំបួន [dorb pram buon]
2	ពី [pee]	20	ម្ភៃ [mpay]
3	បី [bay]	21	ម្ភៃមួយ [mpay muoy]
4	បួន [buon]	22	ម្ភៃពី [mpay pee]
5	ប្រាំ [pram]	30	សាមសិម [sam sep]
6	ប្រាំមួយ [pram muoy]	40	សែសិម [sae sep]
7	ប្រាំពី [pram pee]	50	ហាសិម [haa sep]
8	ប្រាំបី [pram bay]	60	ហុកសិម [hok sep]
9	ប្រាំបួន [pram buon]	70	ចិតសិម [chet sep]
10	ដប់ [dorp]	80	ប៉ែតសិម [paet sep]
11	ដប់មួយ [dorb muoy]	90	កៅសិម [kao sep]
12	ដប់ពី [dorb pee]	100	មួយរយ [muoy roy]
13	ដប់បី [dorb bay]	1000	មួយពាន់ [muoy poan]
14	ដប់បួន [dorb buon]	10,000	មួយម៉ឺន [muoy muen]
15	ដប់ប្រាំ [dorb pram]		
16	ដប់ប្រាំមួយ [dorb pram muoy]	½	មួយភាគពី [muoy paek pee]
17	ដប់ប្រាំពី [dorb pram pee]	¼	មួយភាគបួន [muoy paek buon]

NOTES

MARCO POLO TRAVEL GUIDES

MARCO ⊕ POLO

With ROAD ATLAS & PULL-OUT MAP

FRENCH RIVIERA
NICE, CANNES & MONACO

SPECTACULAR GRAND CANYON DU VERDON
Breath-taking scenery that takes some beating

SNIFFING THE AIR
The perfume manufacturers of Grasse

Travel with Insider Tips

www.marcopolo.com

MARCO ⊕ POLO

With STREET ATLAS & PULL-OUT MAP

NEW YORK

MEADOWS, WILD FLOWERS AND SKYSCRAPERS
so chic: the High Line in Chelsea

COCKTAIL ON CLOUD NINE
rooftop bar at 230 Fifth Street

Travel with Insider Tips

MARCO ⊕ POLO

With ROAD ATLAS & PULL-OUT MAP

AKE GARDA

NTE BALDO WITH MOUNTAIN BIKE
car in Malcesine takes bikes too

SSES" IN SALO
chocolate "Lucerti"

Travel with Insider Tips

MARCO ⊕ POLO

With STREET ATLAS & PULL-OUT MAP

BERLIN

A STUNNING ISLAND JUST FOR ART
howcasing treasures from around the world

COOL AT NIGHT
club scene sets the trend

Travel with Insider Tips

MARCO ⊕ POLO

With ROAD ATLAS & PULL-OUT MAP

ALLORCA

AN FLAIR IN THE MEDITERRANEAN
Mallorca's most beautiful beach

"IN" CROWD MEET
onda in Deià

Travel with Insider Tips

- PACKED WITH INSIDER TIPS
- BEST WALKS AND TOURS
- FULL-COLOUR PULL-OUT MAP
  AND STREET ATLAS

ROAD ATLAS

The green line ▬▬ indicates the Trips & Tours (p. 98–103)
The blue line ▬▬ indicates The perfect route (p. 30–31)

All tours are also marked on the pull-out map

Photo: Women traders on Tonle Sap Lake

Exploring Cambodia

The map on the back cover shows how the area has been sub-divided

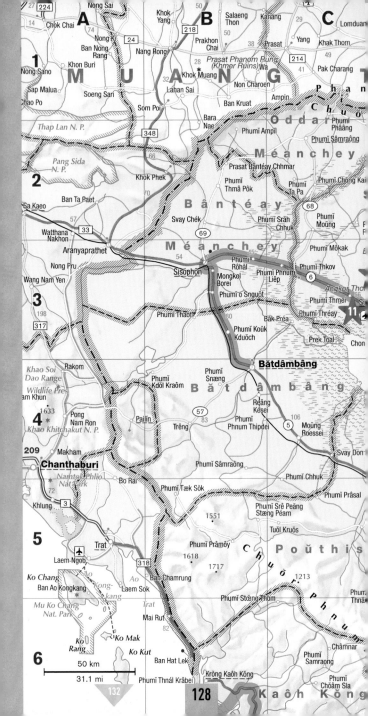

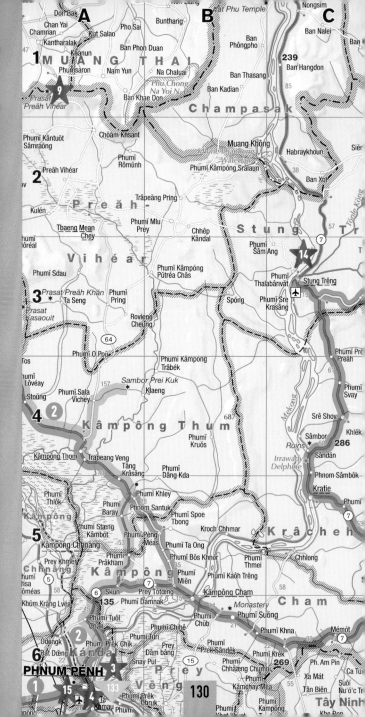

Grid references: A, B, C; rows 1, 2, 3, 4, 5, 6

Don Bak · Chan Yai · Pho Sai · Buntharig · Wat Phu Temple · Nongsim · Ban Nalei · Ban

Chamnan · Kut Salao · Ban Phongpho · Ban Hangdon · Ban

Kantharalak · Ban Phon Duan · **239**

1 MUANG THAI · Khanun · Phumĭsaron · Nam Yun · Na Chaluai · Na Khae Don · Ban Thasang · **85**

Phu Chong · Ban Kadian · Champasak

Na Yoi N. · Prasat Preäh Vihéar · **9**

Phumĭ Kântuŏt Sâmraòng · Chŏăm Khsant · Muang Khôngg · Habraykhoun · Siĕ

2 Preäh Vihéar · Phumĭ Rômünh · Phumĭ Kâmpóng Srâlaun · Ban Xot · **38**

Kulén · Preäh- · Trâpeăng Pring

Tbaeng Mean Chey · Phumĭ Mlu Prey · Chhêp Kândal · Stung · **57** · Tr

humĭ lôréal · Vihéar · Phumĭ Sâm Ang · **14** · **7**

Phumĭ Sdau · Phumĭ Kâmpóng Pŭtréa Chăs · Phumĭ Thalabânvăt · Stung Trêng · T

3 Prasat Preäh Khăn Ta Seng · Phumĭ Pring · Spóng · Phumĭ Sre Krasăng · **19**

Prasat Kasaouit · Rovieng Cheúng · Phumĭ Prè Preäh

Tos · **64** · Phumĭ O Poŭ · Phumĭ Kâmpóng Trâbék · **61**

humĭ Lôvéay · Sambor Prei Kuk · Phumĭ Svay

Stoŭng · Phumĭ Sala Vichey · **157** · Klaeng · Srê Shov

4 **2** · Kâmpóng Thum · **687** · Phumĭ Kruŏs · Sâmbor · Khlĕk · **286** · Mekong

Kâmpóng Thom · Trapeang Veng · Tăng Krâsăng · Phumĭ Dâng Kda · Ruins · Sàndàn

Phumĭ Thlôk · **43** · Irrawady Delphine · Phnom Sâmbôk

Phumĭ Baray · Phnom Santuk · Kratie

Kâmpóng · **28** · Phumĭ Spoe Tbong · Kroch Chhmar · Phumĭ

5 Phumĭ Stæng Kâmbôt · Phumĭ Pěng Méas · Phumĭ Ta Ong · Krâchéh · **7**

Kâmpóng Chhnăng · **53** · Phumĭ Bôs Khnor · Phumĭ Kaôh Trêng · Chhlong

Prey Khmĕr · Phumĭ Prâkham · Kâmpóng · Phumĭ Miĕn · **58**

Chhnăng · Phumĭ Miĕn · Kâmpóng Cham · Cham

humĭ hsa ômếas · **5** · **58** · Skun · **6** · **7** · Prey Tôtœng · Kâmpóng Cham · **58**

Khūm Krăng Lvéa · **135** · Phumĭ Damnak · Monastery · Phumĭ Suŏng

Oŏengk · **2** · Phumĭ Tuôl Chăn · Phumĭ Chihê · Phumĭ Chŭb · Phumĭ Khna · Mémót · **7**

6 Bât Dœng · Kândal · Phumĭ Prêk Chik · Phumĭ Turi · Prey · Phumĭ Prêk-Sândêk · Phumĭ Krêk · Ph. Am Pin · Ca T

PHNUM PÉNH · Dăm bâng · **15** · Phumĭ Chhæng Chumni · **269** · Xa Mát · Suôi

1 · **15** · Snay Pul · Prey · Phumĭ Kâmchay Mea · Tân Biên · Nu'ó'c Tr

· **133** · Phumĭ Prêk Chruk · Vêng · **130** · Phumĭ Kampông · Tây Ninh

· **4** · **1a** · Khmau · Phumĭ · Phumĭ · Kho Don

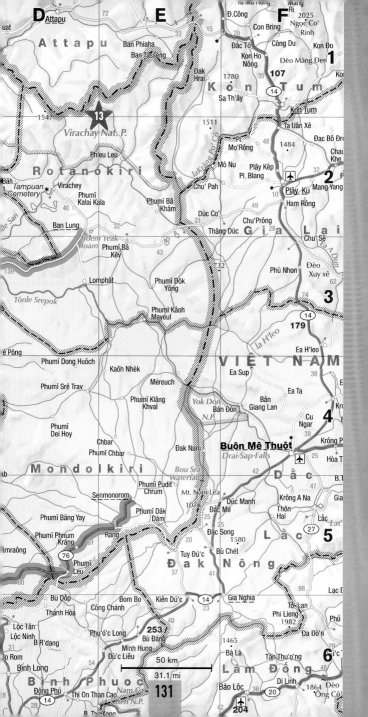

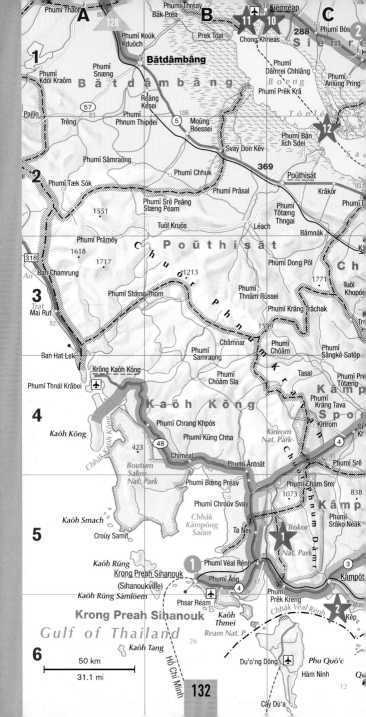

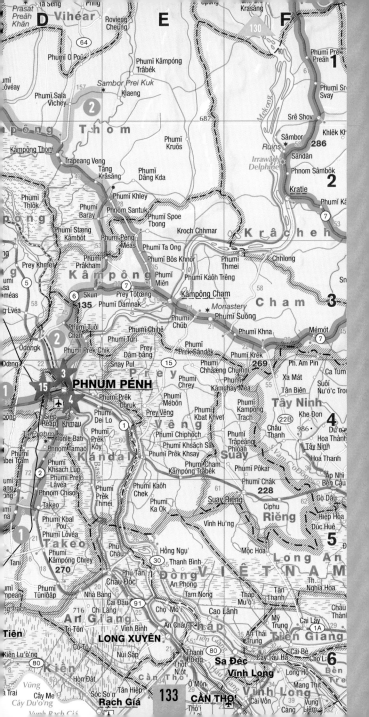

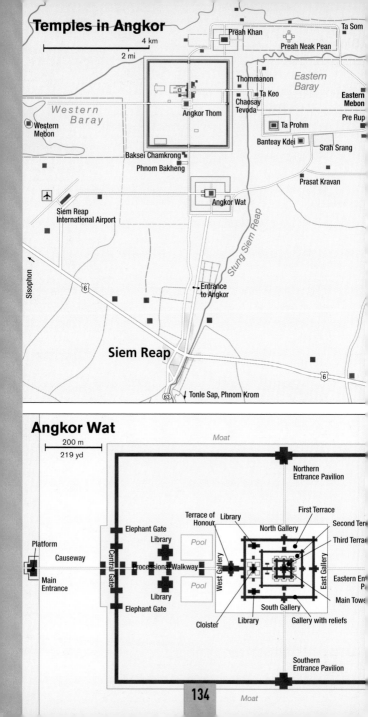

Temples in Angkor

2 mi
4 km

Ta Som
Preah Khan
Preah Neak Pean

Thommanon
Ta Keo
Chaosay Tevoda

Eastern Baray

Eastern Mebon

Pre Rup

Western Baray

Western Mebon

Angkor Thom

Ta Prohm

Banteay Kdei

Srah Srang

Baksei Chamkrong
Phnom Bakheng

Prasat Kravan

Siem Reap International Airport

Sisophon

Angkor Wat

Stung Siem Reap

Entrance to Angkor

Siem Reap

6

6

63
Tonle Sap, Phnom Krom

Angkor Wat

200 m
219 yd

Moat

Northern Entrance Pavilion

Library

First Terrace

Terrace of Honour

North Gallery

Second Terrace

Third Terrace

Elephant Gate
Library

Platform

Pool

Central Gate

West Gallery

East Gallery

Causeway

Processional Walkway

Eastern Entrance Pavilion

Main Entrance

Pool

Main Tower

Elephant Gate
Library

Cloister

Library

South Gallery

Gallery with reliefs

Southern Entrance Pavilion

Moat

134

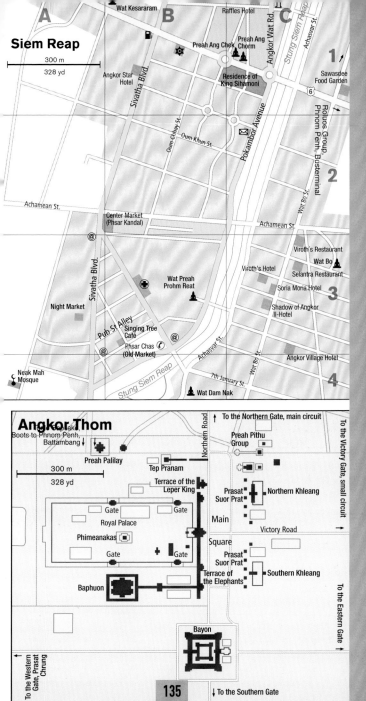

Siem Reap

300 m
328 yd

A · B · C

1 · 2 · 3 · 4

Wat Kesararam
Raffles Hotel
Preah Ang Chek
Preah Ang Chorm
Residence of King Sihamoni
Angkor Star Hotel
Sivatha Blvd.
Oum Chhay St.
Oum Khun St.
Pokambor Avenue
Angkor Wat Rd.
Stung Siem Reap
Achasvar St.
Sawasdee Food Garden
Rolous Group, Phnom Penh, Busterminal
Wat Bo St.
Achamean St.
Center Market (Phsar Kandal)
Achamean St.
Viroth's Restaurant
Wat Bo
Viroth's Hotel
Selantra Restaurant
Soria Moria Hotel
Wat Preah Prohm Reat
Shadow of Angkor II-Hotel
Night Market
Sivatha Blvd.
Pub St Alley
Singing Tree Café
Phsar Chas (Old Market)
Neak Mah Mosque
Stung Siem Reap
Achasvar St.
Wat Bo St.
Angkor Village Hotel
7th January St.
Wat Dam Nak

Angkor Thom

300 m
328 yd

Boots to Phnom Penh, Battambang
Preah Palilay
Tep Pranam
Terrace of the Leper King
Gate
Gate
Royal Palace
Phimeanakas
Gate
Gate
Baphuon
Northern Road
To the Northern Gate, main circuit
Preah Pithu Group
Prasat Suor Prat
Northern Khleang
Main
Victory Road
Square
Prasat Suor Prat
Southern Khleang
Terrace of the Elephants
To the Victory Gate, small circuit
To the Eastern Gate
Bayon
To the Western Gate, Prasat Chrung
To the Southern Gate

135

KEY TO ROAD ATLAS

Autobahn mit Anschlussstellen	Motorway with junctions
Autobahn in Bau	Motorway under construction
Mautstelle	Toll station
Raststätte mit Übernachtung	Roadside restaurant and hotel
Raststätte	Roadside restaurant
Tankstelle	Filling-station
Autobahnähnliche Schnellstraße mit Anschlussstelle	Dual carriage-way with motorway characteristics with junction
Fernverkehrsstraße	Trunk road
Durchgangsstraße	Thoroughfare
Wichtige Hauptstraße	Important main road
Hauptstraße	Main road
Nebenstraße	Secondary road
Eisenbahn	Railway
Autozug-Terminal	Car-loading terminal
Zahnradbahn	Mountain railway
Kabinenschwebebahn	Aerial cableway
Eisenbahnfähre	Railway ferry
Autofähre	Car ferry
Schifffahrtslinie	Shipping route
Landschaftlich besonders schöne Strecke	Route with beautiful scenery
Alleenstr. Touristenstraße	Tourist route
XI-V Wintersperre	Closure in winter
Straße für Kfz gesperrt	Road closed to motor traffic
8% Bedeutende Steigungen	Important gradients
Für Wohnwagen nicht empfehlenswert	Not recommended for caravans
Für Wohnwagen gesperrt	Closed for caravans
Besonders schöner Ausblick	Important panoramic view

Donnortei *Terme di Casteldoria* Sehenswert: Kultur - Natur	Of interest: culture - nature
Badestrand	Bathing beach
Nationalpark, Naturpark	National park, nature park
Sperrgebiet	Prohibited area
Kirche	Church
Kloster	Monastery
Schloss, Burg	Palace, castle
Moschee	Mosque
Ruinen	Ruins
Leuchtturm	Lighthouse
Turm	Tower
Höhle	Cave
Ausgrabungsstätte	Archaeological excavation
Jugendherberge	Youth hostel
Allein stehendes Hotel	Isolated hotel
Berghütte	Refuge
Campingplatz	Camping site
Flughafen	Airport
Regionalflughafen	Regional airport
Flugplatz	Airfield
Staatsgrenze	National boundary
Verwaltungsgrenze	Administrative boundary
Grenzkontrollstelle	Check-point
Grenzkontrollstelle mit Beschränkung	Check-point with restrictions
ROMA Hauptstadt	Capital
<u>CÁGLIARI</u> Verwaltungssitz	Seat of the administration
Ausflüge & Touren	Trips & Tours
Perfekte Route	Perfect route
MARCO POLO Highlight	MARCO POLO Highlight

INDEX

This index lists all places and sights mentioned in this travel guide. Numbers in bold indicate a main entry

WRITE TO US

e-mail: info@marcopologuides.co.uk

Did you have a great holiday?
Is there something on your mind?
Whatever it is, let us know!
Whether you want to praise, alert us to errors or give us a personal tip – MARCO POLO would be pleased to hear from you.
We do everything we can to provide the very latest information for your trip.

Nevertheless, despite all of our authors' thorough research, errors can creep in. MARCO POLO does not accept any liability for this. Please contact us by e-mail or post.

MARCO POLO Travel Publishing Ltd
Pinewood, Chineham Business Park
Crockford Lane, Chineham
Basingstoke, Hampshire RG24 8AL
United Kingdom

PICTURE CREDITS
Cover Photograph: Monks in Angkor Wat, Getty Images/Photographer's Choice: Hellier
Images: Courtesy of KlapYaHandz (16 centre); Ecole d'Hôtellerie et de Tourisme Paul Dubrule (17 top); Getty Images/Photographer's Choice: Hellier (1 top); Huber: Jones (126/127); KeoK'jay: Grant Salisbury (16 top); mauritius images: age (102), Alamy (2 top, 5, 7, 20, 30 l., 86, 88, 89, 91, 92, 95, 97, 114 top), Flüeler (3 top, 84/85), Photononstop (26 r.); M. Miethig (1 bottom); Project AWARE Foundation (16 bottom); O. Stadler (flap r., 2 centre bottom, 2 bottom, 3 centre, 3 bottom, 9, 24/25, 26 l., 28/29, 30 r., 32/33, 50/51, 53, 56/57, 63, 77, 79, 81, 82/83, 98/99, 104/105, 106/107, 111, 114 bottom, 115); Tara Riverboat: Ma. Theresa D. Auxillo (17 bottom); M. Thomas (10/11, 18/19, 27, 43, 48, 58, 60, 67, 69, 100, 101, 103, 108/109, 117); M. Weigt (flap l., 2 centre top, 4, 6, 8, 12/13, 15, 22, 23, 28, 29, 34, 37, 38, 41, 44, 46, 49, 55, 64, 70, 72, 75, 109, 110, 110/111)

1st Edition 2013
Worldwide Distribution: Marco Polo Travel Publishing Ltd, Pinewood, Chineham Business Park, Crockford Lane, Basingstoke, Hampshire RG24 8AL, United Kingdom. Email: sales@marcopolouk.com
© MAIRDUMONT GmbH & Co. KG, Ostfildern
Chief editors: Michaela Lienemann (concept, managing editor), Marion Zorn (concept, text editor)
Author: Martina Miethig, Editor: Cordula Natusch
Programme supervision: Anita Dahlinger, Ann-Katrin Kutzner, Nikolai Michaelis
Picture editor: Gabriele Forst; What's hot: wunder media, Munich;
Cartography road atlas: © MAIRDUMONT, Ostfildern; Cartography pull-out map: © MAIRDUMONT, Ostfildern
Design: milchhof: atelier, Berlin; Front cover, pull-out map cover, page 1: factor product munich
Translated from German by Robert McInnes, Vienna; editor of the English edition: Tony Halliday, Oxford
Prepress: BW-Medien GmbH, Leonberg
Phrase book in cooperation with Ernst Klett Sprachen GmbH, Stuttgart, Editorial by Pons Wörterbücher

DOS & DON'TS ☝

A few things to bear in mind in Cambodia

DON'T THREATEN A THOUSAND YEAR OLD CULTURAL HERITAGE

Accept restrictions on taking photographs and barriers to protect Cambodia's cultural heritage. Don't climb around on the sandstone artworks in Angkor and elsewhere, lean your rucksacks against them and touch everything: this happens thousands of times – every day! – and damages the substance of the objects. And please do not buy any *genuine* artworks or everyday articles used by the ethnic groups for your living room at home.

DON'T GO AROUND HALF-NAKED

Respect the local customs: Cambodia is heavily influenced by Buddhism and is a conservative country. Under no circumstances should you should enter a temple in a miniskirt, strap top or shorts (men and women); take your shoes off before you enter and remove your hat. Monks must not be touched by women. Some sunbathing rules: never topless and never ever nude! It is ok to wear a bikini at Sihanoukville but everywhere else (rivers, lakes, waterfalls and near fishing villages) female tourists should be just as 'decent' as the locals when they bathe – in a sarong or t-shirt and shorts.

DON'T GO OUT ALONE AT NIGHT

You should not go for a walk alone at night anywhere in Cambodia (in any case, it is usually pitch dark because there is no street lighting and the dogs – each Cambodian family has at least one – are an aggressive pack). Women should absolutely not stroll on the beach alone at night.

DON'T GIVE CHILDREN MONEY

Even if their big wide eyes make you weak: do not give begging children any money – their begging is often an organised business and the start of a life-long career in the 'trade'. It is better to make a donation to one of the organisations listed below, visit restaurants where former street children are trained (such as *Friends* and *Romdeng* in Phnom Penh) or orphanages such as *Chres Village School* and *Orphanage* in Siem Reap *(www.cambodianorphan age.org.uk)*. Or buy from the charity shops like the *Cambodian Children Painting Project (CCPP)* in Sihanoukville. Some charitable organisations: *www.friends-international.org, www. sangkheum.org (child centre), www. camkids.org*

DON'T TAKE DRUGS

Forget all the myths you've heard: marijuana is also forbidden in Cambodia! So keep your hands off of any kind of drug – regardless of whether it's *ganja, jaba, Happy Herb Special Pizza* with heady ingredients, or designer pills. By the way, there have been reports of the police set-ups and sometimes the cocaine sold here has turned out to be pure heroin...